NYMPHING
A BASIC BOOK

Stackpole Books

NYMPHING
A BASIC BOOK

Gary A. Borger

Drawings by Robert H. Pils

NYMPHING
Copyright © 1979 by
Gary A. Borger

Published by
STACKPOLE BOOKS
Cameron and Kelker Streets
P.O. Box 1831
Harrisburg, Pa. 17105

Published simultaneously in Don Mills, Ontario, Canada
by Thomas Nelson & Sons, Ltd.

Library of Congress Cataloging in Publication Data

Borger, Gary A   1944-
  Nymphing.

  Bibliography: p.
  Includes index.
  1. Trout Fishing. 2. Nymphs (Insects) 3. Fly
fishing. 4. Flies, Artificial. I. Title.
SH687.B67   799.1'7'55   78-11358
ISBN 0-8117-1010-6

Printed in the U.S.A.

To Nancy,
friend,
angling companion,
confidante,
wife

CONTENTS

	ACKNOWLEDGMENTS	9
	PREFACE	11
Chapter 1	EQUIPMENT	13
Chapter 2	LINE CONTROL	25
Chapter 3	BIOLOGY OF THE TROUT	38
Chapter 4	LIES OF THE TROUT	51
Chapter 5	NYMPHING THE FILM	64
Chapter 6	STRIP/TEASE NYMPH FISHING	78
Chapter 7	OLD STANDBY	88
Chapter 8	CADDIS MANIA	97
Chapter 9	WINGSHOOTING AND THE JUMPING NYMPH	107
Chapter 10	THE LONG TIPPET	116
Chapter 11	STRIKE INDICATORS AND SHOTGUNNING FOR TROUT	123
Chapter 12	SECRET OF THE WOOLY WORM	131
Appendix A	THE DEADLY DOZEN	140

8 Contents

Appendix B KEYS TO SUBAQUATIC FOOD ORGANISMS
OF THE TROUT   159

ANNOTATED BIBLIOGRAPHY   183

ANNOTATED LIST OF REFERENCE TEXTS
AND KEYS USED FOR IDENTIFICATION
OF INVERTEBRATE FOOD ORGANISMS OF
THE TROUT   187

INDEX   189

ACKNOWLEDGMENTS

Special thanks to Him who made it possible.

Bob Pils is an exceptionally gifted illustrator. His fine drawings do much to give depth to this book. For your artistic contributions and many hours of companionship on the stream, my warmest thanks, Bob.

Howard West is a good friend. He has encouraged my writings and generously introduced me to many of his favorite waters. Our discussions have ranged across the full breadth of fly fishing. Howard works for 3M, and both he and the company deserve thanks for helpful background data on fly lines.

Dick Gaumer of Fenwick is another good friend who deserves warm acknowledgments for encouraging and counseling my writings.

Jim Green, master rod designer for Fenwick and unexcelled fly caster, generously offered much information on rod-building materials and their properties. I appreciate his help very much.

Thanks, too, to Nick Lyons, who gave counsel when I was seeking a publisher and to Dave Whitlock, who has patiently listened to many of my ideas and given support to my writings and lectures.

I also want to thank Jerry Hoffnagle, Sales Manager at Stackpole Books, for making *Nymphing* a reality.

To my friends who, over the years, have fished with me and generously shared their insights, thank you.

Some of the material in this book is excerpted from articles written by the author and first appearing in the following periodicals: *Fly Fisherman*, *Roundtable*, Fenwick's *Lunker Gazette*, and *Fly Fisher*. I wish to acknowledge their permission to use this information.

PREFACE

In fly fishing, a nymph is loosely defined as any subaquatic, invertebrate food organism of the trout. Insects come first to mind: the nymphs of mayflies, stoneflies, dragonflies, damselflies, and true bugs; the larvae and pupae of caddises and midges; the larvae of dobsonflies, fishflies, alderflies, beetles, and moths; and adult aquatic bugs and beetles. The smaller crustaceans (scuds and cressbugs) are called nymphs. Leeches, small aquatic worms, and snails also fall into this category. Artificial nymphs, as opposed to classic wet flies, are expressly designed to imitate one or more of these subaquatic forms.

It's a well-worn statement, but tried and true: trout are nymph eaters, spending as much as 90 percent of their feeding time dining on this subaquatic fare. This is especially the case with brown trout. Brooks, rainbows, and cutthroats feed at the surface much more readily than do browns. But even at that, all trout are opportunists and the greatest opportunities for food lie beneath the surface.

Ted Trueblood once said there are two places to fish for trout: on the bottom or at the surface. In large measure this is correct. When a hatch is in progress, the fish feed on the organisms concentrated at the film. Other times food must be sought in the sheltering rubble of the bottom. But occasionally, nymphs will drift in the midcurrents and trout will then feed there. The nymph fisher must possess a range of tactics that not only permit presentation of the fly at different depths but allow the various actions of the naturals to be mimicked. Essential, too, is a knowledge of what the food organisms are and how they react. The way the trout perceives his environment and where he holds in lakes and streams should be clearly understood.

Nymphing has been written with all these factors in mind. The illustrations and information in Appendix B will help in identifying nymphs; Appendix A describes useful artificials, and the first four chapters outline the nymphing tackle needed, the skills of line control, reading the water, and the biology of the trout. This information is integrated into the eight chapters on nymph fishing tactics.

Fly fishing, and nymphing in particular, is more than just a method of catching trout. To me it is an open-ended learning experience with lessons in ecology, entomology, limnology, botany, ichthyology, natural history, and much more. It is a pursuit limited only by the pursuer. My sincere hope is that this book will expand the angling horizons of the reader and thereby increase the pleasures obtained from our matchless sport.

EQUIPMENT

There's a saying among fly fishers that equipment isn't the only thing, it's everything. This tongue-in-cheek poke at our insatiable desire to possess far more rods, reels, and lines than we'll ever need does point up a most important aspect of angling: you have to have proper equipment. It doesn't mean you have to buy the most expensive items available. It does mean the equipment has to be of the most suitable design for the job at hand, in this case, nymph fishing.

RODS

I've never run across any piece of equipment that evokes as much discussion as does the fly rod. At times it is described in purely physical terms as a flexible lever arm moving a certain mass. Other times it takes on mystical qualities that transcend all understanding and is described with a certain awe by its privileged owner. And that's as it should be. The angler ought to understand a bit of the physics of rod design and can only grow more attached to a favorite rod as the years pass.

Today's rods may be bamboo, glass, or graphite. The most important property of these materials is *absolute flexure modulus*. This is a measure of stiffness as related to weight. Glass fibers are light in weight but very flexible; so they have a low absolute modulus. Bamboo fibers are quite stiff but bamboo is heavy; so the absolute modulus is only moderate, though it's better than glass. Graphite is very stiff and light (high absolute modulus); lesser amounts of graphite than either glass or bamboo are necessary to make any given rod. This means a lightweight, thin-diameter rod. The small diameter offers little air resistance; so the rod, and hence the line, can be moved much faster. High line speed gives more control of the cast because the line will be less influenced by wind and gravity. Line speed is also a function of the rate of *recovery* of the rod, i.e., how fast it returns to a straight position from a flexed position. This, of course, depends upon absolute flexure modulus and rod design. Graphite recovers faster than either glass or bamboo.

Bamboo does have excellent *loading properties*. The rod bends to a certain point, but then, even though more load is applied, the bend does not increase significantly. Thus, the fibers release the load very rapidly over the relatively short distance they've been flexed and generate high line speed. The rod flexes about the same amount regardless of the length of the cast. This is the "feel" that anglers like about bamboo. Graphite has very similar loading properties. Glass, however, will continue to bend as the load is applied, and much of its flexed energy is lost in simply straightening out the large bend.

During the casting stroke, the rod does not just return to a straight position from its flexed position. The tip tends to keep going and flexes back and forth several times before coming to a halt. This creates undesirable humps in the fly line—like making snakes in a garden hose. Graphite, because of its great stiffness, has good *dampening ability*, returning to a straight position with very few oscillations of the tip. Bamboo is also good, but glass has poor dampening properties.

Because graphite fibers are so stiff, a rod of this material is more sensitive to vibrations of the line than either bamboo or glass, and sensitivity is what the nymph fisher wants. Graphite, in my opinion, makes the ultimate nymphing rod, but there are fine rods in both bamboo and glass.

The way a rod flexes *during the casting stroke* is called the action. If just the tip flexes, it's a *tip-action* rod. If the upper one-half to three-fifths flexes, it's a *medium-action* rod. When a *full-action* rod is cast, it will flex down to the grip (Fig. 1-1). The medium action is best. If only

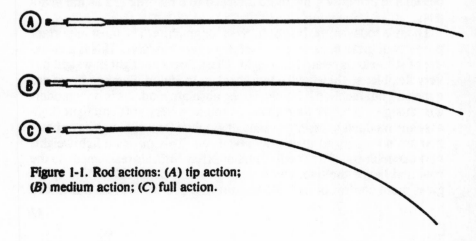

Figure 1-1. Rod actions: (*A*) tip action;
(*B*) medium action; (*C*) full action.

the tip flexes, the rod won't accept much of a load and therefore can't contribute much energy to the cast. When the entire rod flexes, the load is distributed over too much material and recovery is slow. You can readily determine the action of a rod by holding it horizontal and making casting motions out in front of yourself. Watch for the portion of the rod that is flexing.

When choosing a rod, also look at its fixtures. The tip top guide should be chrome-plated wire; a ceramic tip top adds unnecessary weight that robs the rod of energy during the cast. Snake guides should be hard chrome-plated to resist wear and large in diameter to allow the line to shoot freely. I prefer a ceramic butt guide with a 10 or 12 mm opening. Ceramic guides are practically frictionless and the large diameter is necessary to allow free flow of the line. Many rod companies now offer a reverse-locking reel seat. To me, this is the only way to go. The locking nut is back out of the way where your hand won't rub it and loosen it. In addition, the weight of the reel is always against the nut and acts to keep it from loosening (Fig. 1-2).

Rods in the eight- to nine-foot length are best. With shorter rods it's

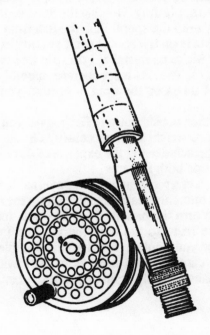

Figure 1-2. Reverse reel seat and lightweight, single-action reel with interchangeable spools.

too hard to hold line off the water. Very long rods are just too tiring to cast pleasurably all day.

REELS

The reel is more than just a place to store line. Even in its cheapest form, the reel is a place to store line *neatly*, provides a convenient method of handling excess line, and allows a refined approach to playing the fish. A finely built reel is not only a pleasure to own, it is a most functional piece of equipment.

Select a single-action reel that has sufficient capacity to hold the fly line and backing. There should be an efficient and smooth drag. For normal trout fishing the drag is not used to apply pressure to the fish; rather, it is used to prevent spool overrun and the resultant backlash. Before fishing, set the drag just tight enough to prevent overrun and then leave it alone. Your finger is a far more sensitive drag than any mechanical system. When playing a fish, keep the line in the first joint of the index finger of your rod hand. Simply bend your finger and squeeze the line to apply drag. Holding the line like this also allows you to guide it evenly onto the spool. Play the fish from the reel whenever possible. If the line is on the reel, it can't get tangled around your legs or other objects. Make no mistake, I do strip line when I have to, but *only* when I have to. The reel must operate smoothly while playing the fish; if the spool binds or the drag is erratic, you're going to have problems.

Weight is another consideration. Each time you cast, you lift the reel. Why lift more weight than necessary? On the other hand, lightness should not be achieved at the expense of durability. A well-made reel will incorporate both features.

By all means select a reel that can be converted for right- or left-hand cranking and has interchangeable spools. Set up the reel so you can use your line hand to turn the handle. This way you don't have to switch the rod from one hand to the other during that most crucial period immediately after you hook a fish. Interchangeable spools allow the nymph fisher to carry two or three extra lines without much added weight and to change rapidly from one to the other.

BACKING

Backing has two important uses. First, it's an indicator. When the backing starts out through the guides, it's time to take after the fish.

Backing is also insurance. If you get into a big trout up at Ruby Creek Campground on the Madison, he may well decide to head down to Ennis Lake. You've got to have enough backing to let him make his run while you get out onto the bank and make your run. The best backing material is 20-pound test, or heavier, braided dacron line. It will not rot and does not stretch. Braided nylon is a second choice because it stretches. Use 50 to 100 yards of backing; you don't often need it, but when you do, you do!

LINES

Modern fly lines are made by applying a plastic coating to a braided nylon or dacron core. Level lines (L) have a uniform diameter throughout their length. As early as the middle of the last century anglers understood that a level line turned over too forcefully for delicate presentations, splashing down onto the water and spooking the fish. By tapering the last ten feet or so of the line, delicate presentations could be achieved. Double-tapered lines (DT) have a taper at each end. A weight-forward line (WF) consists of the first thirty feet of a double-tapered line followed by a thin-diameter running line. Shooting-head lines (SH) are essentially the same as a weight-forward, but the running line is monofilament (Fig. 1-3).

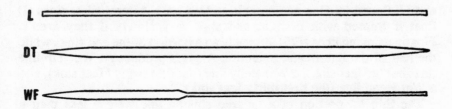

Figure 1-3. Line tapers: *L*, level; *DT*, double-tapered; *WF*, weight-forward.

A fly line is also categorized according to the weight of its first thirty feet. This length is used because it is the average casting distance (Table 1-1). A number four, or occasionally a three, is useful for midge fishing. Big weighted nymphs are easier to handle on six- and seven-weight lines. I consider a five-weight to give the best all-around performance.

Table 1-1. American Fishing Tackle Manufacturers Association (AFTMA) fly line categories. Weights are in grains (437½ grains=1 ounce) for first 30 feet of line.

Line Number	Weight	Plus or Minus Allowance
1	60	6
2	80	6
3	100	6
4	120	6
5	140	6
6	160	8
7	185	8
8	210	8
9	240	10
10	280	10
11	330	12
12	380	12

Floating lines are designated with an F. Sinking lines (S) come in various densities and hence various sink rates. Scientific Anglers, for example, makes four sinking lines: Wet Cel I is a slow-sinking line, Wet Cel II sinks at a moderate rate, Wet Cel Hi-D is a rapid-sinking line, and Hi-Speed Hi-D is comparable to lead core. Intermediate lines (I) float if treated with floatant and sink very slowly if they aren't. Floating/sinking lines (F/S) are made so a portion of the end sinks while the rest of the line floats. Scientific Anglers produces a Wet Tip line (the first ten feet sink), a Wet Belly line (the first twenty feet sink), and a Wet Head line (the first thirty feet sink).

The thin tip portion of a tapered sinking line weighs less than a similar length from the middle of the line. Upwelling turbulence near the stream bottom (see chapter 4) can lift the lighter tip easier than the heavy midsection. Thus, that part of the line that should be closest to the bottom is often buoyed a significant distance above the bottom. Charlie Brooks recommends in *The Trout and the Stream* that for bottom bouncing with nymphs in deep, fast currents, a level line is better than a tapered line. It's sound advice. An additional benefit is that the level line can turn over big weighted nymphs easier than can a tapered line.

Floating lines should be tapered to deliver the fly softly. Both double-taper and weight-forward lines are acceptable. Remember that the first thirty feet of a WF is the same as the first thirty feet of a DT and that the front tapers are identical. It's the remainder of the line that's different.

A weight-forward is made for distance casting; however, it will not roll cast much beyond forty feet because the thin running line cannot carry enough energy to turn over the heavy head. The weight-forward line has an advantage over the double-taper when it comes to putting it on the reel. The thin running line of the WF takes up far less room on the spool than does the heavy belly of a DT. For this reason, you can get by with a smaller, hence lighter, reel and still have plenty of capacity for backing.

Lines made with a sinking tip are useful for nymphing where the fly doesn't have to get down really deep. Since the belly floats, it can be readily mended to prevent drag on the fly. There are nymphing tactics that will allow the same presentation without the use of this special line. There are also very specialized sinking-tip lines and sinking/floating-tip lines that are useful in nymph fishing; they are discussed later in this chapter.

ROLLING YOUR OWN

The *long head line* was first used by Edward Hewitt in the 1930s. It takes advantage of the best properties of the double-taper and weight-forward lines. Lee Wulff has popularized this design in recent years, and Garcia Corporation has one on the market. For my long head lines, I cut a level or double-tapered line in half and splice it onto half a shooting line (Fig. 1-4). Scientific Anglers manufactures a fine shooting line. It is .029 inch in diameter, floats, and comes in fluorescent orange. The finished long head line will allow roll casts to sixty

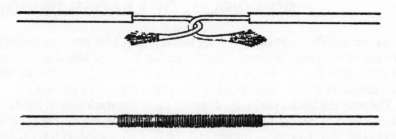

Figure 1-4. Splicing fly lines. Remove coating from 1¼ inch of each line, fray ends and cut to point, fold over each other, whip with thread, and coat with Pliobond cement.

feet. For a standard cast, if you get that long head out of the guides and let her go, it's not too hard to reach 100 feet. This type of line also allows the use of a smaller reel than would a level or double-tapered line.

For fishing big weighted flies near the bottom in fast currents, a *lead-tip line* works very well. A four- to six-foot piece of either 36-pound test lead-core line or a number 15 Hi-Speed Hi-D line is spliced to a shooting line. Remove the lead core from that part of the line used to make the splice. The shooting line is the key to the success of this outfit. Its fine diameter allows the angler to shoot line easily, mend with little effort, and hold line off the water without undue strain. In addition, the small diameter minimizes drag. Mending and strike detection are further aided by the floating nature and high visibility of the shooting line.

In *Fly Fishing Strategy*, Doug Swisher and Carl Richards suggest using short pieces of lead-core line (six inches to a couple of feet) between the fly line and leader to help get the fly down. Make loops on either end of the lead-core line (strip the plastic finish, remove the lead wire, and whip a loop on the end). These short lead tips can then be added or removed as need be. This is a good way to get flies down in all but the big, deep, fast runs and pockets. There a lead-tip line is more effective.

A rather interesting opposite to these lead tipped heavyweights is the sinking/floating-tip line. Myron Gregory, who was instrumental in establishing the AFTMA system of fly line designations, described such a line in *Fly Fisherman* magazine (vol. 9, no. 2, 1978). It seems that Myron's friend Ben Fontaine was nymphing in a deep Belgian lake and kept catching the bottom vegetation. By splicing the front taper of a floating line to the tip of a sinking line, the problem was alleviated.

PRINCIPLES OF LEADER DESIGN

As the terminal part of fly fishing tackle, the leader not only delivers the last bit of energy that casts the fly, but once on the water affects the way in which the fly moves and the rate at which it sinks. Give particular attention to the leader; this is one place it pays to be fussy.

The way the leader performs depends upon the thickness of the butt, the stiffness of the material, the overall length of the leader, the relative lengths of butt to taper to tippet, and the fly being used. A heavy, stiff butt will deliver more energy to the fly than a thin, limp one. But, as Doug Swisher and Carl Richards point out in *Fly Fishing Strategy*, if the material is significantly stiffer than the fly line, the casting loop will open as it reaches the leader—like trying to cast a stick on the end of a string.

Maxima, Nylorfi, Kroic G. T., and Aeon (also sold under the Creative Sports label) have about the same stiffness as the fly line. Nylorfi and Kroic G. T. have phenomenal strength per diameter and are very limp; however, they tend to lose their stretch and become scored after several hours of hard fishing—especially in the last few inches of the tippet. When used, these materials should be checked frequently and replaced at the first sign of scoring. Aeon is also very limp and very strong, but so far I have not had a chance to thoroughly evaluate it under angling conditions. Maxima is slightly stiffer than the others, but does not become scored as easily when fished. For these reasons, I use Maxima for most of my leaders, falling back on the others when extra limpness or greater strength is needed, especially in the very small diameters. The moderate stiffness of Maxima also allows it to carry more energy per diameter. Regardless of the material you choose, be sure to measure its diameter with an accurate micrometer; manufacturing labels can be incorrect.

Thick-butted leaders are fine for large flies but don't present tiny flies with delicacy or allow a rapid sink rate. On the other hand, a very light butt will not carry enough energy to cast a big fly. The solution is to balance butt diameter and leader design to the fly and the tactic being used. I use four different butt sizes (Table 1-2).

Table 1-2. Leader Formulas. Select the leader with the overall length and tippet and butt sizes required. The diameter and length of each segment of the leader can then be read directly from the chart. Note that there is a selection of tippet sizes for each leader. The last segment of the tapered portion may also be used as a tippet; in this case the length is indicated in parentheses.

Segment Lengths (inches)

Leader Design:	Magnum		Standard		Midge		Ultra-Midge	
Overall Length:	100″	150″	100″	150″	100″	150″	100″	150″

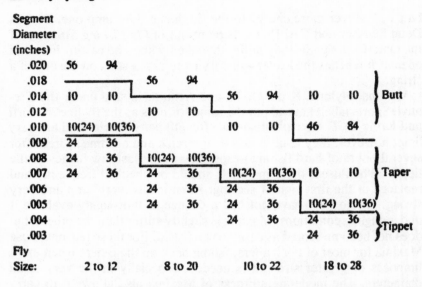

Segment Diameter (inches)	2 to 12		8 to 20		10 to 22		18 to 28		
.020	56	94							
.018			56	94					Butt
.014	10	10			56	94	10	10	Butt
.012			10	10					
.010	10(24)	10(36)			10	10	46	84	
.009	24	36							
.008	24	36	10(24)	10(36)					
.007	24	36	24	36	10(24)	10(36)	10	10	Taper
.006			24	36	24	36			
.005			24	36	24	36	10(24)	10(36)	
.004					24	36	24	36	Tippet
.003							24	36	
Fly Size:	2 to 12		8 to 20		10 to 22		18 to 28		

There can be as much as a thirty percent difference in the diameters of adjacent segments of the leader before "hinging" occurs at the knot. One of the problems with this large reduction in diameter is knot slippage. The surgeon's knot and Stu Apte's blood knot hold well when connecting materials with large differences in diameter, but I prefer my double blood knot (Fig. 1-5) since it is more streamlined than the others and just as strong and secure.

To the end of the fly line I nail knot a 10-inch-long connector of .020-inch diameter leader material, then tie a perfection loop in the

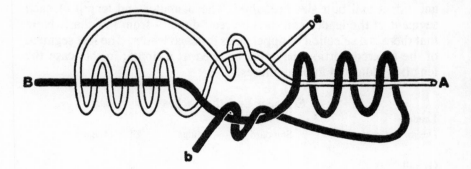

Figure 1-5. The double blood knot. Take three turns with each strand outside the knot and one inside. Pull *A* and *B* to tighten outside loops; then pull *a* and *b* to tighten inside loops.

loose end of the connector. A perfection loop on the butt end of the leader allows rapid changing of leaders (Fig. 1-6). The .020 connector also allows attachment of leaders with butt diameters as small as .014 inch.

Note that the leaders given in Table 1-2 can accept up to four different tippet diameters. In addition, by extending the tapered sections of the Magnum, Standard, and Midge series with .007, .005, and .004, respectively, they will accept even smaller tippet diameters. The leaders may also be modified by increasing or decreasing the length of butt, tapered section, tippet, or all three. These adjustments allow the angler to balance not only leader with fly but the entire system to angling tactics and water and weather conditions.

Commercial tapered leaders are fine, but you should add your own tippets. Also measure them with a micrometer to be sure of butt size. They can be modified by shortening the butt, lengthening the tippet, or both.

MISCELLANEOUS ITEMS

Be sure to take along a pair of tan, polarized sun glasses on your fishing trips. Tan is best for both bright and overcast days, and the polarized lens allows you to see into the water. If you can see the fish, your chances of catching it are significantly increased. Also take a stomach pump. This rubber bulb suction device is the best way to obtain a stomach sample without killing the fish. When you know what they're taking, catching them is certainly less difficult. Use it properly. Fill with water, insert carefully so as not to damage the gills, pump a *little* water into the stomach, then vacuum out the contents. Take along collection equipment such as a surface screen, vials, hand lens (10X), small tweezers, and a white plastic saucer for examining and collecting trout food. A stream log is vital. It allows you to keep accurate records on hatch dates and locations, an invaluable aid to consistent angling success. Other handy items include micro-shot, removable BB-size split shot, moldable lead putty, a pair of scissor pliers (great for pinching down the barb, putting on shot, trimming a fly, etc.), a 10X monocular, a flex light, and hook hones.

Equipment may not be the only thing, or everything, but the proper tools sure make nymphing easier and more pleasant.

Chapter 2

LINE CONTROL

If you took all the various ingredients of fly fishing—casting, fly tying, entomology, stream craft, equipment, standard fishing fables, and so on—put them in a pot and boiled them, then collected, condensed, and bottled the very essence of the sport, you'd have to call it *line control*. For all the blood, sweat, and tears of fly fishing lead to that one moment of putting the fly over the fish—correctly.

Presentation (the art of making the fly seem alive to the fish) is the ultimate skill in line control. The nymph fisher must be a consumate artist in presentation, able to present the fly at any depth. If the natural floats dead drift just below the surface, then to be most effective, the artificial must do likewise. Trout may be intercepting insects that are rising from the bottom to the surface; the successful angler will imitate this behavior with his fly. The food organism may be crawling in the bottom rubble and the trout may refuse all presentations except the one that mimics this crawling movement, and so on.

There is nothing mystical about good line control. It means being able to select the right casting technique, cast the fly accurately, and handle the line correctly once it's on the water. You should concentrate on learning the basic casts, mends, and ways of handling the line rather than trying to learn a specific presentation for every possible angling situation. These fundamental tactics should be so well understood as to be automatic. There is no time to think of what your hands should be doing when you have to be watching the line or leader for a strike. Murphy's Law applies in nymph fishing more than in any other method: big fish always hit when you're not paying attention.

In addition to positioning and manipulating the fly so it seems alive, the nymph fisher must control the line sufficiently to be able to detect strikes and pull the hook home. Casting, mending, and line handling techniques should be chosen to *continuously minimize* the *unnecessary* slack in the line. Alvin Grove, in his fine book, *The Lure and Lore of*

Trout Fishing, perfectly describes the allowable slack as no more "than can be taken up immediately with the lifting of the rod tip in setting the hook. . . ." Make this your credo.

Such tactics as the reach cast, parachute cast, double haul, tension cast, curve cast, mending in the air, and so forth are not just neat fly rod tricks; they are essential to nymph fishing. If you are unfamiliar with any of these techniques, study the appropriate section below and practice until the cast is yours. Work on it for a month or so, taking a half hour to practice it on the stream each time you go fishing.

BASIC CASTING STROKE

All casts are built on the basic casting stroke. If you practice it until it is automatic, all the casts are easily within your command. The method I use is that of Fenwick rod designer and international casting champion Jim Green. His book, *Fly Casting from the Beginning,* is a masterful study of the subtleties of casting.

Grip the rod with your thumb on or near the upper side, fingers curled around comfortably. The wrist is relaxed and allowed to tip forward so that the rod is an extension of the forearm. Start with your arm at your side and the rod parallel to the ground (Fig. 2-1).

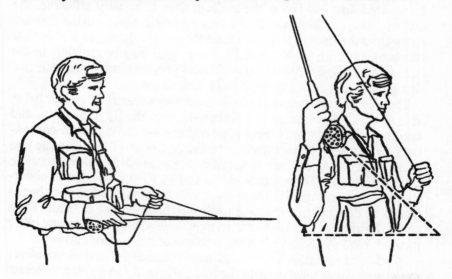

Figure 2-1. Beginning of basic casting stroke. Rod is an extension of the forearm and parallel to the ground.

Figure 2-2. Rod lifted to twelve. Note paths hand and elbow follow.

First, raise your arm *without bending your wrist* until your hand is back even with your shoulder and about as high as the side of your face. You will have to *raise your elbow* slightly as your arm comes back. Your hand follows a straight path from its initial point to where it stops. This path is at about forty-five degrees to the ground (Fig. 2-2). Notice the rod; it should be pointing nearly straight up (twelve o'clock).

Second, *after* stopping at twelve, relax your wrist and allow the rod to fall back until it is pointed to about one or one-thirty (Fig. 2-3). This

Figure 2-3. Drift with rod. This is *not* a power stroke.

Figure 2-4. Forward cast. Hand moves forward, *as* elbow drops, and finishes with a flip.

is not a power stroke; it's a *drift* with the rod that allows a longer movement on the forward cast.

Third, with your wrist still bent back, move your forearm forward while *simultaneously dropping your elbow*. Your hand should move down along the same 45-degree path that it followed when you raised the rod. When your forearm is pointing to ten o'clock, stop hard and snap your wrist forward to flip the tip of the rod (Fig. 2-4).

ROLL CAST

Start with the rod parallel to the water. Raise your arm *slowly* and stop at twelve. The line will slide toward you on the water. If you lift too fast, the line will jump off the water rather than slide along the surface. When the line gets to you, relax your wrist and let the rod drop back to one or one-thirty. Then move forward to ten and flip the tip. The line will form a loop and roll out across the water (Fig. 2-5). This is

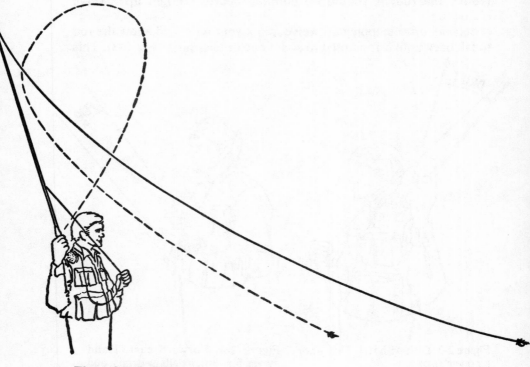

Figure 2-5. Roll cast.

a useful cast for the nymph fisherman. The line is not aerialized so you can fish when there is brush close behind you. Also, the nymph is not dried out by the cast and will sink readily. This cast can be used to pick up a floating line and to get a sinking line up onto the surface in preparation for other casts.

OVERLAND ROLL CAST

When fishing spring creeks or lake edges, it is sometimes necessary to stay fifteen to twenty feet back from the water. Obstructions close behind may dictate a roll cast. Grasp the bend of the hook with your line hand and shake the necessary line out through the guides. Make a roll cast, but stop the rod high. As the line snaps off the ground, release the fly. The line will roll forward high, straighten, and settle gently to the water.

PICKUP AND LAYDOWN CAST

Begin with your arm held comfortably at your side and the rod parallel to the water. Lift with a *smoothly accelerating* motion—don't allow your wrist to bend—and *stop sharply* at twelve o'clock. The rod will cast the line out behind at an angle of about twenty degrees above the horizontal (Fig. 2-6). *Don't* apply power by bending the wrist. Such

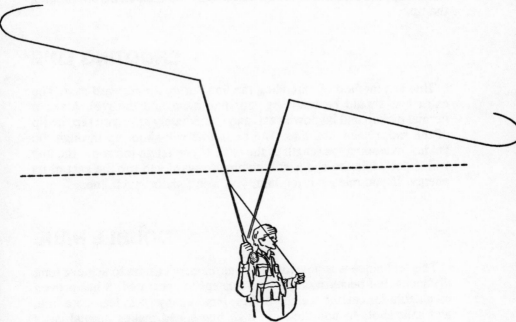

Figure 2-6. Pickup and laydown cast.

a motion usually results in sweeping the rod back past twelve, throwing the line downward behind. After the stop, relax the wrist and allow the rod tip to drift back.

When the line is almost straightened behind, begin the forward cast. Start slowly, accelerate smoothly, and stop sharply. If you start the cast with a sudden jerk rather than a smoothly accelerating motion, the line jumps suddenly, causing it to tangle, catch the rod tip, or snag an ear. This is the most common fault anglers make when executing the forward cast. It's called kicking.

Hold the forearm at the ten o'clock position until the line has entirely straightened in front. The arm can then be lowered to follow the line down. This will result in a quiet settling of line, leader, and fly to the water's surface.

LOOP CONTROL

When the loop is formed at the ten o'clock position, it will be narrow and fast-moving and will cut into even the strongest winds. To form a wide loop, the forearm is brought down to nine o'clock before flipping the tip.

SHOOTING LINE

This is a method of extending the line during the forward cast. The extra line should be between your line hand and the reel. Make a normal pickup and laydown cast, and immediately *after* you flip the tip of the rod, release the line. The extra line will shoot up through the guides, extending the length of the cast. If you let go too soon, the line will shoot while the rod is still coming forward and rob the cast of its energy. If you release it too late, you won't shoot much line.

DOUBLE HAUL

This technique was developed by tournament casters to achieve long distances, but because of the high line speed generated, it has proven invaluable for casting weighted flies, large bushy flies, lead-core line, and split shot. In addition, the high line speed makes normal casts almost effortless, even into the wind.

In this cast, the line hand pulls on the line just at the moment when the line loop is formed. On the backcast this would be when the rod reaches twelve o'clock. On the forward cast, the pull comes when the arm stops and the rod tip is flipped. If the pull comes too soon—for example, as the rod starts forward—the effect of the haul is lost. In fact, it can "kick" the line if done improperly and become more of a hindrance than a help. Rod hand and line hand must work together (Fig. 2-7). The most important thing to remember is to haul *when the loop is being formed,* not before, not after.

Figure 2-7. Double haul. The pull *must* be made when the loop is formed.

REACH CAST

In *Fly Fishing Strategy*, Doug Swisher and Carl Richards describe the reach cast as one of the most important casts in fly fishing. For the nymph fisherman, this is doubly so. The reaching technique allows the most advantageous positioning of the line and minimizes unnecessary slack.

After you've stopped the rod on the forward cast, tip the rod out to the side until it is horizontal. You can extend the reach by pushing the rod out to the side as far as you can. The line loop will travel straight to its original target, but the reach will position the line out to one side (Fig. 2-8). The reach can be made on either side of the body.

MENDING IN THE AIR

Mending can be defined as changing the attitude of the line after the forward line loop is formed. Mends can be made when the line is lying on the water's surface or while the line is still in the air. A mend in the air and to the right is made by twitching the rod tip to the right and then

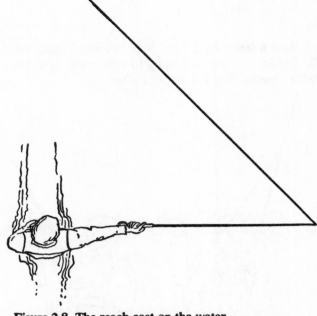

Figure 2-8. The reach cast on the water.

back to its original position. A mend to the left is made by twitching the rod tip to the left. The twitch must come after the forward loop is formed. The strength of the twitch determines the size of the mend.

Rather than make a straight cast and then correct it immediately after it falls to the surface, mend in the air so the line falls to the water already mended. Mending in the air is also useful for casting ahead of rocks lying straight upstream from you. Cast over the rock; then mend so the line falls to one side.

S-CAST

This is just a series of in-the-air mends made one immediately after the other. The rod tip is jiggled back and forth, creating a series of right- and left-hand mends. Currents must pull out all the S-shaped bends before drag occurs. This cast is very useful, but try to avoid getting too much slack in the line.

MENDING ON THE WATER

In order to mend on the water, there must be some slack in the line. This is usually introduced with an S-cast or in-the-air mend. If you've made a straight cast and need to mend, feed some line through the guides to provide necessary slack. Raise the rod horizontally to lift the necessary amount of line up off the surface; then flop it where you want it. Try to do this as smoothly and carefully as you can to avoid pulling the fly around.

PARACHUTE CAST

If the line is cast downstream, drag will occur the moment the fly touches the moving water. Some people use the S-cast to overcome this drag, but the slack will be floating *away* from you and make hooking and strike detection very difficult. Charles Ritz described a cast in his book, *A Fly Fisher's Life*, that is perfect for downstream angling. The parachute cast is made by pulling the rod back to twelve just after the forward cast is made. Do not jerk it back or make a backcast; the correct movement is just a gentle pull. The entire line will move toward you in the air, then drop to the surface. The line is lying straight down stream and the rod is pointing straight up in the air (Fig. 2-9). By

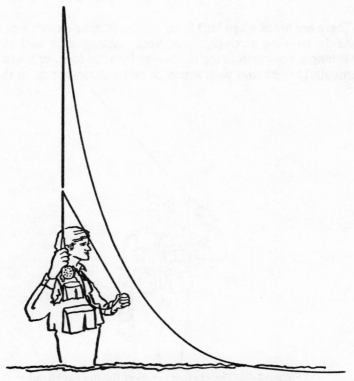

Figure 2-9. A just completed parachute cast.

simply lowering the rod tip, the line is permitted to float downstream at the same rate as the current, totally eliminating drag and slack.

TENSION CAST

This is more of a pitch than a cast. Suppose you're dredging with heavily weighted nymphs fished on a lead-tip line, casting up and letting the fly bounce along the bottom. When the fly gets downstream, lift the rod about shoulder high and let the current force the line to the surface. The rod should be pointing downstream. Now, sweep the rod upstream, keeping it parallel to the water, and make a forward cast. The drag of the line on the surface will load the rod, and when you make the horizontal forward cast, the line and fly will be pitched neatly upstream.

BACKHAND CAST

There are times when backhand casting is quite useful, e.g. when the wind is blowing strongly from your casting side and the line is threatening your well-being as it zings by your face, or when fishing a particularly tight spot with brush or other obstructions on the normal

Figure 2-10. The correct position for the backhand cast.

casting side. The backhand cast is also used for making curve casts. Hold the rod upright at the twelve o'clock position; now tip your wrist toward your head but keep your arm in its normal casting position. The rod will be tipped over the top of your head, and the line will be on the line hand side of your body (Fig. 2-10). The backhand cast is made by *keeping your wrist tipped* and simply running through the normal casting sequence; the rod will move back and forth over your head. Any of the casts described above can be performed with the rod in this backhand position.

CURVE CASTS

Like the reach cast, the curve drops the line to one side of the fly to compensate for variation in current flow or to prevent spooking a fish. If the line loop is formed with excessive energy, then after the line straightens, the extra energy drives the leader on over, causing it to curve downward. This is the principle behind the overpowered curve. For a positive overpowered curve, tip the rod out to the side and flip the rod tip extra hard when forming the loop. The loop will flip over and curve toward your line hand. The curve can be accentuated by pulling the rod tip back sharply for several inches immediately after forming the loop. For a negative overpowered curve, tip the rod as described for the backhand cast. The line will roll forward and curve away from your line hand.

If the cast is made without the flip, the line will go out a few feet and collapse in a heap. This is the principle behind the underpowered curve. It is used to cast large, heavy flies or very long leaders. Tip the rod out to the side and simply sweep it slowly forward in an arching motion. The line loop will be large and will fall to the water in a sloppy curve away from the line hand. The positive underpowered cast is made in the same way, but a backhand cast is used. This underpowered curve is hard to cast accurately and creates a large amount of slack; it should be used only when absolutely necessary.

LINE HANDLING

These are procedures that are followed regardless of the nymphing procedure, casting method, or mending technique. When shooting line, form an "O" with the thumb and index finger of the line hand and allow the line to flow through this ring (Fig. 2-11). As soon as the cast settles,

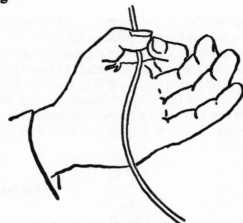

Figure 2-11. The O-ring used when shooting line.

simply close your hand around the line. Instant control! Once the line is down on the water, you should immediately be ready to retrieve extra slack or strike a fish. Make it a habit to put the line under the index finger (or another finger if it feels more comfortable) of your rod hand as soon as the line settles to the water (Fig. 2-12). But don't look down at your hands and lose visual contact with the cast. If the O-ring is

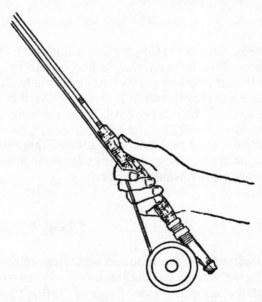

Figure 2-12. Line under the index finger gives instant control.

used, all you need do is put your hands together and transfer the line from one hand to the other.

Always retrieve the line from *behind* the finger of your rod hand. Don't reach up ahead of the rod hand and catch the line, pull it back, and put it under your finger again. Such motion is likely to cause you to look at the rod rather than watch the line on the water. If you always strip from behind the finger of your rod hand, all you have to do to find the line is put your hands together. If a fish strikes, the line is under control; simply tighten your finger on the line and lift the rod.

Make the O-ring/index finger pull sequence a habit, an automatic response to each and every cast. All your efforts can then be directed to watching the line and detecting the strike.

ACCURACY

Accuracy is achieved by practice, but not unless the casting stroke is correct. That's why I make such an issue about learning the fundamentals of casting. Here are some tips for improving accuracy.

(1) Learn the basic casting stroke. Do it correctly and do it until it is automatic. Do it the same way every time.

(2) Learn to control loop size. A small, fast-moving line loop can be cast more accurately than a big, slow-moving loop.

(3) Use the same casting plane for both the backcast and forward cast. Don't take the rod straight back and then let it fall out to the side on the forward cast.

(4) The line goes where the rod tip goes. You aim the line by aiming the tip. If you don't know what the rod tip is doing, you don't know where the line is going.

(5) Keep your casts as short as possible. Not only will the casts be more accurate, but you'll be able to see the rises better and keep excess slack out of the line easier.

(6) Know your equipment—what the rod can and cannot do, what the line contributes, how leader design affects accuracy, and what roles fly size and construction play.

Chapter 3

BIOLOGY OF THE TROUT

VISION

The trout's eye is designed very much like that of other vertebrates. Light passes through the cornea and pupil and is focused by the lens onto the retina (Fig. 3-1). However, the pupil is fixed in size; consequently, the fish can't adjust its eyes to the brightness of the light. Ray Bergman reasoned that a fish near the surface and looking at a floating fly against the sun would, thus, see the fly less distinctly than if it were in the shade. His angling experiences proved him correct. If you experiment with flies in the sun, be very careful that the shadow of the line doesn't fall across the trout and spook it.

The lens of the trout's eye is oval with its long axis lying parallel to the long axis of the body. Focusing is accomplished by moving the lens back and forth along its long axis. Because the eyes are placed in the

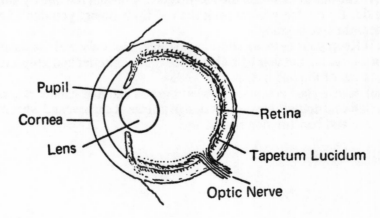

Figure 3-1. Structure of trout's eye.

sides of its head, the fish has a field of view of about 330 degrees; however, because of the way its eyes focus, objects less than 3 feet away are seen clearly only straight ahead in a narrow 30-degree field (Fig. 3-2). In this area of focusable vision, the trout can see objects so close they almost touch the eyeball. Its maximum visual range is de-

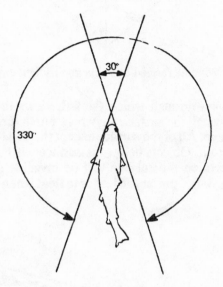

Figure 3-2. The trout's fields of vision.

termined by the distance light travels through water; in fresh water this is about forty feet. Peripheral vision (to the sides of the area of focusable vision) is unclear from the fish's eye out to a distance of about three feet. Beyond that the trout's sight is good and very sensitive to contrast and motion. When a fish is out in the open feeding, it knows it is exposed to danger and will usually be frightened by a sudden movement in the area of its peripheral vision.

When passing from air into water, or vice versa, light rays are bent (refracted). The amount of bending is determined by the angle at which the light strikes the surface. If the rays strike perpendicular to the surface, no bending occurs. Rays entering horizontally are bent at 48.5 degrees from the vertical.

Light rays can enter the water from any direction, upstream, downstream, or from the sides, and as they pass through the surface and to the trout's eye, they are funnelled by refraction into a cone having an apical angle of 97 degrees (Fig. 3-3). Thus, there is a circular

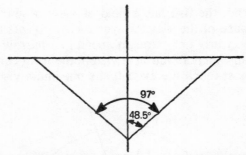

Figure 3-3. Window formed by refraction as light enters the water.

area—the *window*—through which the fish views the outside world. Light coming through the surface anywhere but in the window will not reach the fish's eye. All of the surface except the window will appear as a mirror to the trout. Objects below the surface will be reflected in this mirror and objects on the surface will be invisible unless they're in the window (Fig. 3-4). I prefer the leader to float when nymphing on the

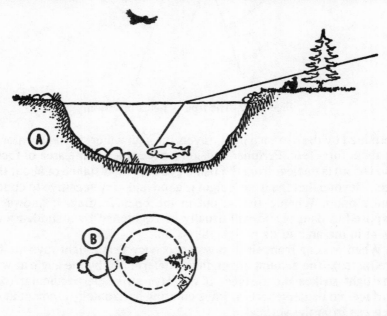

Figure 3-4. Trout's view through the surface. (A) Fish looking at surface. Man and part of tree are within the ten-degree angle of indistinct vision. (B) View fish has of surface. Man and lower part of tree indistinct (rim of indistinct vision not to scale). Bird plainly visible. Rocks reflected in surface are seen just at edge of window.

surface and try to present the fly, when possible, so the leader will be upstream of the window. This way the fish will not see it or see it only very poorly.

When a fish looks through its window, it is literally looking around a corner; however, the object does not appear to be around a corner. The fish sees the object along the same line that light enters its eye. Likewise, when an angler sees a fish, the fish appears along the same line that light enters the angler's eye (Fig. 3-5). Unless you're looking

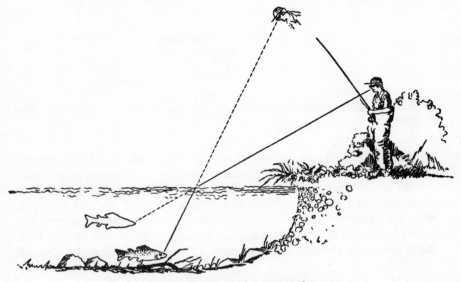

Figure 3-5. Refraction and apparent images.

straight down on it, the trout will always be *deeper* and *closer* than it appears to be. The deeper the fish is, the more this distortion occurs. For this reason, always cast on your side of the fish; by doing so you're actually casting to the fish.

Light fades rapidly with depth and objects above the surface quickly become hard to see. Unless the water is very clear, trout near the bottom in deep pools are usually not watching the surface; they're watching the bottom. Fish feeding at the surface are usually high in the water and focusing their attention above the surface. They are very likely to notice the uncautious angler. Then, too, when out in the open feeding, the trout will be far more alert to danger than when lying deep near the protective bottom.

Many rays striking the water at less than ten degrees above the horizontal skip off the surface. This creates the glare that polarized glasses so effectively block. Thus, the light coming in under ten degrees will be less bright to the fish than the light entering the rest of the window. In addition, these low-angle rays are compressed very close together by refraction (Fig. 3-6). This means the horizon is jammed down into a thin, shadowy image that occupies the outer rim of the

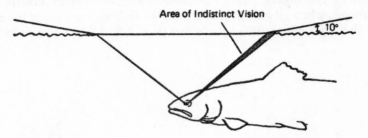

Figure 3-6. Objects under ten degrees are indistinct and compressed very close together; to scale.

window (Fig. 3-4). At 30 feet from the trout, the 10-degree margin reaches up to 5 feet 3½ inches, and the largest share of your body would be quite indistinct to the fish. To get closer than 30 feet, you must stay low to keep within the 10-degree angle. At 15 feet you shouldn't present more than 2 feet 7¾ inches of yourself above the surface. So, it's down on the old hands and knees. If you're on a high bank along the stream, you may have to crawl on your belly. Use all

Figure 3-7. Keeping low to get close to the trout.

available streamside vegetation for camouflage. Either approach from behind it or keep it directly behind you, and move slowly.

In rough water, the window is still there, but it changes shape and moves around with the waves. Where there are standing waves, as in riffles or rapids, the trout looks out through the troughs between waves. Its upward vision is greatly reduced by the waves, and in such places, the angler can work close to the trout without being seen. The most difficult visual situation for the trout occurs when a light breeze ruffles the water. The tiny waves move across the surface and refract light in all directions, effectively blocking the fish's view.

Trout have learned to compensate for all the peculiarities imposed upon them by refraction. In fact, they take advantage of it to help them intercept organisms floating on the surface. An insect sitting on the surface pushes the film down slightly. This depression scatters light, producing a sparkling silhouette that is characteristic of the particular insect. This scintillating depression is the first view the fish has of the insect as it approaches his window. Eventually, it will see the insect up on the surface. The highest features of the insect (upright wings, for example) will become visible first. The insect will appear to be up in the air along the line that light enters the trout's eye. As the insect gets closer to the window, more of it becomes visible, and it appears to move down the line of sight. When it reaches the edge of the window, the fish will see it in entirety, and it will look as though it has just touched the surface. Meanwhile, the trout will see the sparkling depression get closer. At the edge of the window, the depression and the insect will come together.

The trout uses this split image to lock in on the insect during the rise. As he rises higher in the water, his window gets smaller, but by keeping the organism at the upstream edge of the window, the trout is following precisely the correct path for interception. All he has to do is open his mouth when he gets to the surface; the organism will be just in front of his nose. When fishing on the surface, place the artificial far enough upstream so that the fish can lock in on it as it approaches the window. The upstream edge of the window is 1.13 times the distance from the trout's eye to the surface (Figure 3-8). To drift the fly naturally into the window of a fish lying twelve inches below the surface, you'd have to cast at least fourteen inches ahead of him.

Trout drift downstream tail first under the organism, watching it closely before finally deciding to complete the rise. In a *simple rise*, the fish drifts a few inches to a couple of feet, pokes his nose out of the water, and takes the fly. During a *compound rise*, the trout not only drifts with the organism but also tips its body vertically, eventually

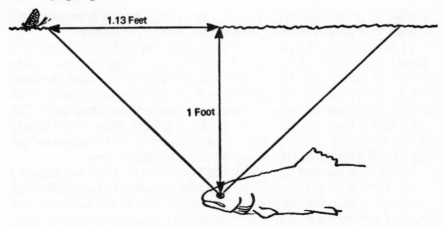

1.13 Feet

1 Foot

Figure 3-8. Dimensions of window.

rising straight up. A *complex rise* occurs when the fish drifts as for a compound rise, seems to reject the fly, then turns suddenly and moves downstream to seize it. These rise patterns and characteristics of the fish's vision are documented in a series of most beautiful photographs in Vince Marinaro's book, *In the Ring of the Rise.* Regardless of the rise pattern, the fish drifts downstream. After the rise, he moves back *upstream* to his lie. Watch the fish rise a time or two to locate his lie. If you cast to the ring, you'll be casting behind the fish.

The retina of the trout's eye contains both cone cells (which see bright light and colors) and rod cells (which are used for night vision). Recent evidence points to the fact that the arrangement of rods and cones in the retina provides what we would consider a rather poor image. They detect form and size, but not detail. However, contrast enhancement and motion perception are heightened. Angling experiences bear this out. If trout formed good images, they'd never take our crude flies. On the other hand, fish often reject a fly because it is the wrong size or shape or because of unseen drag (motion so slight we can't detect it). Trout definitely see color and can see further into the violet region of the spectrum than can man. Fish conditioned to accept one color of food will not feed on other colors of food. Fish trained to separate colors, then shapes, can separate colored shapes easier than just the colors or the shapes alone. Selectivity, then, is a function of color, shape, size, and motion (or lack thereof).

Rod cells cannot see color; so the fish is color-blind at night. Otherwise, trout have good night vision. It is aided by a highly reflective layer, the *tapetum lucidum,* that occurs behind the retina (Fig. 3-1).

This mirrorlike surface reflects light back through the rods, increasing their effectiveness by 40 to 60 percent.

HEARING

In air, sound is a series of compression waves. Water, however, can be compressed only slightly, and here sound takes on two forms; one is a compression wave, and the other is a rippling effect such as that generated by a stone thrown into the water. The ripples don't usually travel more than a couple of hundred feet, if that. The compression waves, however, travel long distances and do so at a mile a second, five times faster than in air. Also, their intensity is not decreased nearly as much as that of sound in air.

Trout have sensory organs that detect both types of underwater sound. The air bladder and inner ear mechanism detect the compression waves much the way our ears detect sounds in the air. The rippling motion of the water is detected by the lateral line system. The line is most noticeable along the sides of the fish (Fig. 3-9), but it also extends

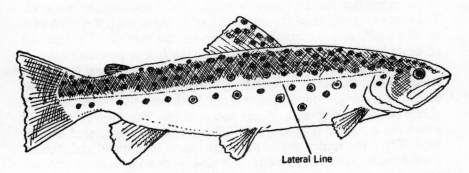

Lateral Line

Figure 3-9. Lateral line.

forward around the eyes and jaws. It consists of a series of openings that connect to a canal below the skin. Nerve endings line the canal (Fig. 3-10). Ripples enter the canal and stimulate the nerves. During swimming, the lateral line also senses distortion in the water flowing along the body. In this regard it is like a radar system; for example, it enables the fish to "feel" the presence of the aquarium glass and avoid bumping into it. Fish may lose their eyes, as some cave fish have, but not their ears and lateral lines. And while trout hunt largely by sight, it is often their hearing that has first alerted them to the presence of a

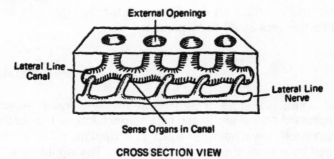

Figure 3-10. Anatomy of lateral line.

food organism. A wiggling nymph or the sound of other fish feeding is readily detected by the trout. At night or in muddy water, lateral line hearing plays a large role in food capture.

The trout's hearing is sensitive from a low of about 15 Hz. to a high of possibly 10,000 Hz. Man's range is 20 to 20,000 Hz. Up to about 1,000 Hz. (two octaves above middle C) their hearing is more acute than ours, but they are far less sensitive to high-frequency sound. This is not surprising, for the watery world is one of low-frequency sound. The careless grinding of the angler's foot in the gravel, the clink of a wading staff, and the scraping of feet on the bottom of a boat all generate low-frequency sounds that alert the fish to potential danger. Many anglers do well in riffles, but fail in the pools and quiet flats. One reason is that the gurgling, splashing water of the riffles helps hide the noises of wading. Sound carries from earth into the water, and the clump of boots along the bank can spook nearby fish. However, sound generated in water is louder than a similar sound generated on the bank. Thus, the angler should not wade unless necessary, and then he should wade cautiously, quietly, and slowly. Sounds in the air do not enter the water unless they are of explosive force; so talking won't bother the fish at all.

SMELL AND TASTE

The nasal passages of the trout are U-shaped tubes (Fig. 3-11). Water enters the forward opening and passes out the rear opening. Inside the chamber, the olfactory rosette senses molecules in the water. It is sensitive enough to detect some molecules in concentrations as small as one in a hundred billion (man's limit is one in a billion). Fish can recognize the smell of other fish and distinguish be-

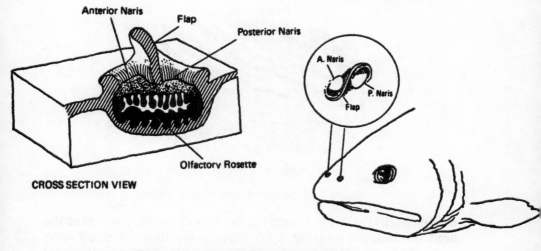

Figure 3-11. Structure of trout's nostrils.

tween species. An injured or frightened fish releases an alarm substance from its skin that other fish can smell; a trout would investigate a minnow's alarm smell but become frightened at another trout's alarm smell. Trout and salmon are repelled by the smell of mammal skin, including man's. Handling the fly will get your scent on it, and though this scent soon washes out of the fly, some anglers wipe sardine oil or anise oil on their hands to cut the human odor.

Taste buds occur over the entire inside of the mouth (they're especially dense on the roof), the gill cavity, gill arches, and lips. In order to taste, the fish need only touch the object with his lips. A fish nudging the fly may actually be tasting it. Trout dislike the taste of gas, oil, or insect repellant. Be careful not to get such materials on the fly.

TOUCH

A trout's skin consists of a thin epidermis overlying a much thicker dermis. Mucous glands in the epidermis continually secrete slime which serves as a first line defense against pathogens. Scales are embedded in the dermis and serve as mechanical protection. When a scale is lost, a new one is formed in its place. Nerve endings occur in the dermis; these are sensitive to touch (Fig. 3-12). If you handle a fish *gently*, it usually won't struggle, but squeezing it will cause alarm. Grip the animal around its midsection, fingers under the belly and thumb

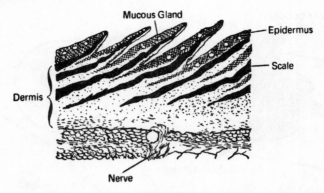

Figure 3-12. Sectional view of trout's skin.

over its back (Fig. 3-13). Cradle big fish in both hands, one behind the head, one near the vent (Fig. 3-14). Don't worry about taking off some of the fish's slime, but don't knock off any scales and be very careful not to get your fingers into the gills.

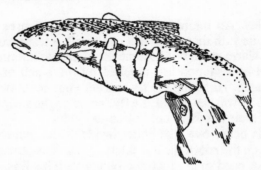

Figure 3-13. Holding trout gently in one hand.

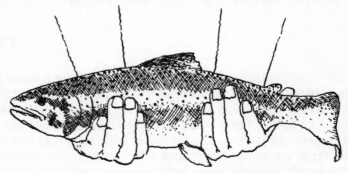

Figure 3-14. Large fish are held in both hands.

FIN AND MUSCLE ARRANGEMENT

The power, speed, and maneuverability of the trout are due to its streamlined shape and fin and muscle arrangement. Fins on the midline of the body provide horizontal stability, while the paired pelvic and pectoral fins give vertical stability (Fig. 3-15). A fish swims by un-

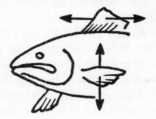

Figure 3-15. Fin arrangement provides both horizontal and vertical stability.

dulating its body, pushing against the water on one side then the other (Fig. 3-16). Its muscles are arranged in chevron-shaped groups that maximize this lateral thrust. When playing a fish, your objective is to tire its muscles. With very light tackle this requires time and careful

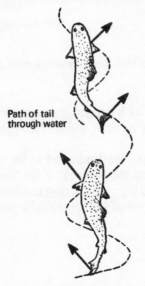

Path of tail through water

Figure 3-16. Fish swims by generating lateral thrust against water. Arrows indicate direction of thrust.

handling to prevent the fish from becoming frightened and breaking the tippet. As soon as you pull the hook home, drop the rod tip to ease the pressure. When the fish calms down, apply gentle pressure by pulling the rod back *parallel to the water*. This way, each time the fish undulates its body away from you, it must work against the rod. Keep the pressure light, but constant, and hold the rod so it forms a large, smooth bend. If the trout becomes alarmed, slack off and give it a chance to relax, then resume gentle pressure. Try to keep the fish on as short a line as possible so you have control; on a long line it can saw around wherever it wants. When the trout runs, drop the rod and point it straight down the line to remove all drag caused by the guides. If the fish is running over weeds, however, get the line high and out of the water to prevent a snag, but keep a smooth bend in the rod (Fig. 3-17). When the fish stops, go after it and get it on a short line again. If it goes

Figure 3-17. Keeping the rod high and smoothly bent as the trout runs over weeds.

into the weeds, back it out with careful pressure. If the trout heads for a snag, try to get in front of it; then splash the water to spook the fish away from it.

The trout is a *wild* animal, well adapted to its watery environment. The angler that understands the biology of the trout will stalk the fish just the way a hunter stalks big game, using available cover and staying out of sight, moving slowly and quietly to take the greatest advantage of each cast.

Chapter 4

LIES OF THE TROUT

Water is a surprising fluid. It's called the universal solvent because it dissolves so many substances. It has an extremely high surface tension which forms a tough, flexible film that can support large insects such as water striders or trap small terrestrial insects that fall into the water. Tiny aquatic insects that emerge at the surface may have difficulty breaking through the film.

Water in lakes and streams is transparent, but not perfectly so. Dissolved substances in the water, algae, and the water itself rapidly absorb light. Usually, plants cannot get enough light to live at depths much greater than forty feet. Food production, then, occurs in rather shallow water, and this is the region where most animal life will be found.

Water is pulled downslope by gravity, forming lakes and flowing to the sea as streams. The land drained by a particular stream is called its watershed. A stream not only shapes the watershed, but draws its very sustenance from this land through which it flows. Minerals and organic matter from the land are carried into the stream by surface runoff and ground water. Algae and higher aquatic plants use the dissolved minerals and sunlight to synthesize food. The invertebrate animals, from single-celled protozoa to insects and crustaceans, feed on the plants and the organic drift from the land. Trout, in turn, feed on the invertebrates (Fig. 4-1).

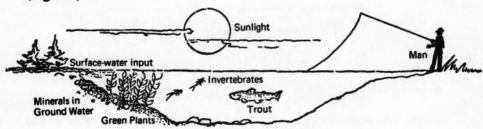

Figure 4-1. The food web in aquatic systems.

A stream is a dynamic system that changes with time. Flowing water tends to form a meandering channel, cutting first against one side, then against the other. Deep holes are formed on the outside of the bends and material is deposited on the inside (Fig. 4-2). Midway between bends is the crossover point where the current swings across the

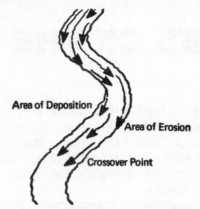

Area of Deposition

Area of Erosion

Crossover Point

Figure 4-2. Meanders in a stream.

stream. This area is usually much shallower than the bend because the current is spread across the entire stream. Meanders provide far greater variation in habitat than does a straight channel. There's often an undercut on the outside of the bend, silt beds on the inside, deep water, shallow water, areas of uniform flow, areas of differential flow, areas of erosion, areas of deposition. Such a wide range of living conditions means a greater variety of organisms can inhabit the area. The classic riffle/pool sequence is another common river configuration, and like the meander pattern, it provides far more variety in habitats than does a simple channel.

In any given stream the current is not uniform from bank to bank or

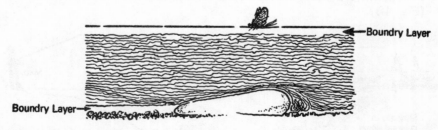

Boundry Layer

Boundry Layer

Figure 4-3. Boundary layers (hydraulic cushions) occur at the bottom and surface.

from top to bottom. Immediately next to the channel is a boundary layer of water (the hydraulic cushion can be a fraction of an inch thick in rapids to a few feet thick in deep, slow-moving pools (Fig. 4-3)). Water at the surface is slowed, to a small extent, by air drag. In a U-shaped channel, the fastest current will be in the center and just below the surface. At a bend, the fastest current is displaced toward the outside (Fig. 4-4).

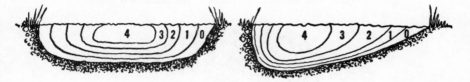

Figure 4-4. Water velocities as seen in cross section of stream: (*A*) straight channel; (*B*) at a bend. The higher the number, the greater the velocity.

While its overall movment is downstream, the water is actually flowing in many directions. This occurs because the slower-moving water at the sides and bottom is sucked into the faster-moving water. As this water flows toward the central current, other water moves in to replace it. Circular eddy currents are thus established (Fig. 4-5). Movement of water in an eddying fashion is called turbulent flow. Water flowing in streams is always turbulent.

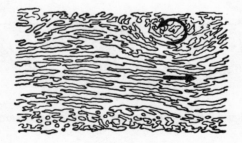

Figure 4-5. Eddy currents at stream edge.

The most noticeable eddies are the reverse currents at the head of a pool (Fig. 4-6) and those on the inside of bends (Fig. 4-7), but eddying occurs all along the banks and bottom of the stream. Bottom eddies result in a general upwelling of water (Fig. 4-8). In rapids, air is mixed into the water, further increasing the upwelling effect. This upward

Figure 4-6. Reverse currents at the head of a pool.

Figure 4-7. Reverse current at a bend.

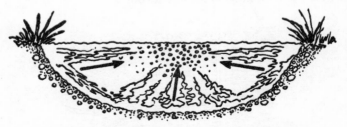

Figure 4-8. Upwelling turbulence in the stream.

flow is of great concern to the nymph fisher since it tends to push the fly to the surface.

Where there's an abrupt change in the vertical drop of the streambed, as at the base of a waterfall, turbulence creates a *standing wave* (Fig. 4-9). This same phenomenon occurs when the current strikes an obstruction in the streambed. If the current is moving rather fast, a standing wave is generated over the downstream edge of the object. These are the waves you see in rapids. They don't move

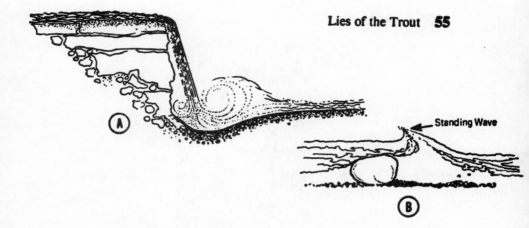

Figure 4-9. Standing waves: (*A*) at base of waterfall; (*B*) at downstream edge of rock (current flow is from left to right).

downstream; rather, they remain always at the obstruction. If the current is slow, or the structure quite far below the surface, the up-welling water only creates a boil or rough spot. By noting the surface characteristics, the angler can gain valuable insights into the positions and sizes of bottom structures.

Trout cannot brave the currents for long without becoming exhausted; so they've learned to take shelter in every nook and cranny where quiet water occurs. They must also seek protection from preda-tors. In fact, the instinct for bodily preservation far outweighs the biological needs to eat and reproduce. Quiet water spots that afford protection from the current and predators are called *sheltering lies*. Areas where the fish can feed, but which offer little or no protection, are strictly *feeding lies*. The ideal spot provides both shelter and food simultaneously; this is a *prime lie*. The best fish will inhabit the prime lies. Reading the water is really a matter of recognizing the areas where these different lies occur.

The best places to find trout are what Tom Wendelburg has called *edges*—where calm water areas meet the currents, where shallow water meets deep water, where the bank and obstructions meet the currents. It's here that drifting food organisms tend to be concentrated. Trout are too large to take advantage of the thin hydraulic cushion in rapids; so they avail themselves of the lies afforded in the lee of rocks and vegetation (Fig. 4-10). From these spots they can watch the current edge and dash out to grab any drifting food organisms. Since the sur-face is usually choppy, the fish feels quite secure, and unless the water is very shallow, these places are prime lies. Fishing the rapids is really

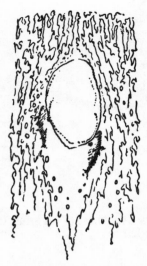

Figure 4-10. Trout holding at edges in lee of boulder.

a matter of "picking the pocket," locating the quiet water areas and drifting your fly along their edges (see chapter 12).

Riffles are slower than rapids and formed where shallow water dances over a stony bottom. The surface will be very choppy because of all the small standing waves. The rubble bottom provides the greatest possible number of niches for the trout and his food organisms, and the moving water brings a continuous flood of oxygen and nutrients into the area. Fish will feel very secure under the choppy surface, and if the water is at least a couple of feet deep, the entire riffle should be considered a prime lie. The best angling tactic is a careful and thorough coverage of the whole area (see chapter 11). Shallow riffles are feeding lies. Fish move into these places during dawn, dusk, and at night.

A run is a deep slot in the channel where current speed is brisk. The surface varies from rather smooth to choppy. Quite often there will be a run within a riffle area. Pockets are broad, nearly circular, deep spots in a riffle. These spots are big trout country (Fig. 4-11). Pay special attention to such water, probing it diligently with bottom bouncing tactics and big nymphs (see chapter 12).

Pools offer a variety of lies. There is a prime lie at the head of a pool; fish hold just underneath the current where it shoots over the lip of the pool (Fig. 4-12). In this lie they're feeding on organisms dislodged in the rapids above and drifting near the bottom. Nymphs fished to these trout should be representative of riffle insects such as stoneflies, fish-

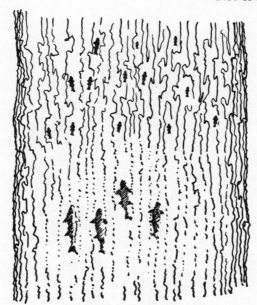

Figure 4-11. Trout holding in riffle and pocket in riffle.

Figure 4-12. Trout feeding in prime lie at head of pool.

flies, and the fast water caddises and mayflies. The fly must come down close to the bottom. For heavy flows, one of the tactics described in chapter 12 will be necessary. In moderate flows the long tippet tactic (chapter 10) is often very successful.

The reverse currents at the sides of pools are excellent places to find trout. With sufficient water depth or plenty of bottom cover, these places will be prime lies. The circulating water traps and concentrates drifting organisms which ride around and around like figures on a carousel. Trout face *into* the reverse current (Fig. 4-13) and work both

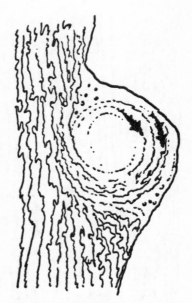

Figure 4-13. Trout watching for food in reverse current.

the bottom and the surface. The most difficult aspect of fishing these spots is to prevent the fly from dragging. The width of the reverse current is often narrow and the water around it is quite still. You just have to be careful.

The pool proper is an interesting assortment of lies. First and foremost it is a sheltering lie; the pool's depth is a comfort to big, predator-conscious fish. Pools are also the winter havens for trout, and in early spring before the trout disperse, the knowledgeable angler will concentrate on these deep water areas. The strip/tease nymphing tactic is superb for probing the depths of pools (see chapter 6). Fish may feed at the surface in the center of the pool if the current is not too strong; otherwise, the feeding lies will occur just at the edges of the current. The best fish will be well up in the pool where the reverse currents join the main current.

During a hatch or after dark, fish will often back down into the tail of the pool and take up feeding positions. Trout defend these feeding lies as a territory, chasing away any smaller fish foolish enough to come too close. Trout will return to their selected feeding spots time after time. Once you locate the lie of a good trout, you can be sure of seeing him there again. If frightened, trout lose all territorial instincts and exhibit schooling behavior. If you spook a small trout in the tail of the pool and it races for cover, the bigger fish will become spooked and dash off. They all head for the depths of the pool where they huddle together in a frightened mass. For this reason, you've got to be especially careful about fishing the tail of a pool. You must practice all your crafts of caution and select your casting and angling approaches before you make the first cast. If there are small fish between you and a large fish, try to catch the small ones and release them downstream so that they won't spook the larger ones.

Bend pools offer the same lies as pools on straight stretches, but in addition, they frequently have an undercut bank on the outside of the bend. Undercuts are prime lies. The quiet turbulence near the bank provides shelter from the current, while the overhanging bank gives the fish protection from predators. Currents concentrate food right at the front door. It's a very cozy setup for the trout. Undercuts can also occur next to strong reverse currents or along straight stretches where sod-covered banks slump into the stream. In woodlands, the water often undercuts the roots of streamside trees. Terrestrial vegetation overhanging the water can be considered an undercut area, and aquatic plants such as water cress often grow over the surface, forming a roof for the trout. These areas may be either prime lies or just feeding lies, depending upon water depth and the amount of cover afforded (Figure 4-14).

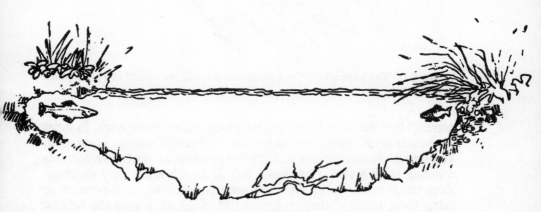

Figure 4-14. Undercuts and overhanging vegetation afford good protection.

The plunge pool at the base of a falls also has sheltering, feeding, and prime lies. There is a quiet water pocket near the bottom immediately under the falling water. This is a prime lie. Trout are perfectly protected from the current and predators, while the falls serves as a conveyor line to bring them food. You've got to get the fly down on the bottom, but the effort is often well rewarded. Reverse currents, the pool proper, and the tail are all handled as for any pool.

The line of convergence where two currents meet is an excellent place for trout. Such spots occur downstream from islands, very large boulders, the pier of a bridge, and where a feeder creek joins the main stream. If the water is at least a couple of feet deep, this confluence line is sure to be a prime lie. Turbulence produced by the meeting of the two currents makes the surface choppy and slows the water markedly. Food organisms flow in from both directions and are concentrated in this quiet water area.

The edge where a still-water slough meets the currents of the stream is another prime lie (Fig. 4-15). Drifting organisms will wash out of the

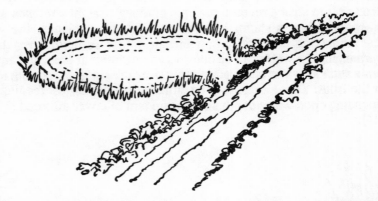

Figure 4-15. The edge where the stream meets a still backwater is a good place to find trout.

currents into the slow water and be concentrated at the edge. In quiet backwater areas, there are often extensive beds of aquatic vegetation. The weeds are comparable to high-rise apartments, with invertebrates dwelling at all levels. Obviously, fish find such areas easy pickings. They cruise rather than hold in one position since there is no current to bring them food. If they're threatened, they duck into the weeds. Weedbeds should always be considered prime lies and every care given to fishing them (see chapter 9). Weedbeds also occur in the stream proper. There, where there is current flow, the vegetation produces the same kinds of sheltered areas as any other obstruction. When the weeds grow up through the surface, there are often pockets of open water scattered through the bed. Trout will frequently lie in these pockets.

A lake is just a stream that isn't going anywhere. It has a watershed that supplies it with water and nutrients; it may be fed and drained by a stream or it may depend entirely upon ground water seeps and intermittent flow from snow melt and precipitation. The web of life is the same in lakes and streams. Green plants harvest the sun and are eaten by insects, crustaceans, and food fishes which in turn serve as fodder for the trout. Lakes even have currents. These are mostly generated by the wind. It piles the water up against the leeward shore and thus promotes a general circulation of water. The horizontal movement of the wind-induced currents propagates vertical turbulence. In this way, oxygen and nutrients are continually circulated in the upper lake waters (Fig. 4-16). True, these currents are not usually as powerful as

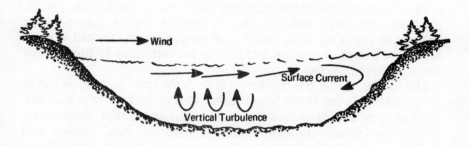

Figure 4-16. Currents in lakes caused by winds.

stream currents, but they can be. Strong winds can cause rips and undertows of immense strength. It is the large surface area, depth, and lack of a constant, unidirectional current that gives lakes their particular characteristics.

Lake habitats can be divided into three usually well-defined regions. First is the *littoral zone*. It is the shoreline region that extends outward to the deepest water where plants can grow. A shallow lake may be entirely littoral. In deep lakes, the dark bottom region in the center where plants cannot grow is called the *profundal zone*. The open water area into which sunlight penetrates is the *limnetic zone* (Fig. 4-17). Obviously, most life in the lake occurs in the littoral and limnetic zones.

The littoral zone is really the zone of rooted vegetation. Emergent plants such as cattails and bulrushes grow along the shore. Farther out

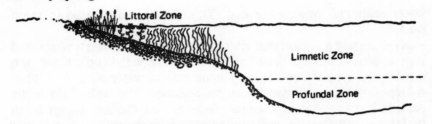

Figure 4-17. The three zones of lakes.

there are floating leaf plants like water lily and pondweed. Submerged plants fill out the remainder of the littoral zone. Elodia, hornwort, and stonewort are frequently encountered submerged plants. Of course not every lake or every area of the lake will display all three types of plant forms. In some spots the shoreline may be marshy and taper off gradually into deeper water; here all three forms can be seen. Other places, the banks are rocky and drop rapidly into the depths; here only the submerged plants are seen. Beaches of sand or gravel exposed to wave action are free of vegetation, but farther out there may be floating leaf and submerged plants.

The life forms that are of interest to both the trout and the fly fisher occur, by and large, in the littoral zone. This is the zone of most light, most oxygen, and most vegetation. Here the damselflies, dragonflies, mayflies, caddises, stoneflies, midges, waterboatmen, beetles, and moths mingle with the scuds, cressbugs, crayfish, and minnows. Trout cruise the openings in the weeds or actively root in search of food. The littoral zone is a nymph fisher's paradise (see chapters 6 and 9).

The limnetic, or open water, zone contains planktonic organisms—the microscopic, free-drifting plants and animals such as algae, diatoms, water fleas, and so on. The half-inch-long larva of the phantom midge (*Chaoborus* spp.), with its transparent body and two dark air sacs, is the only insect to inhabit the open water zone. In very deep, bowl-shaped lakes, the limnetic zone may be the most productive in terms of numbers of organisms. In such lakes the trout will often feed on the tiny organisms of this zone. During a hatch, adult and immature insects are often blown out into the limnetic zone. Trout readily pursue them.

The profundal zone, although dark and often oxygen-deficient, will usually have excellent populations of midges. The pupae of these bottom-dwelling midges come to the surface during the dusk, night, and dawn hours or on overcast days. When they hatch *en masse*, there are literally thousands of them moving through the littoral zone. The surface film concentrates them since the insects must pause there to complete their molt. Trout cruise just under the surface, gorging themselves on the copious insects. The greased leader tactic is the most effective way to fish midge pupae at the film (see chapter 5).

In streams, the current brings food to the waiting fish, but in lakes the fish must cruise in search of things to eat. Thus, there are not specific lies in the lake where trout will hold. However, there are general areas where the trout cruise in search of food. Weedbeds are the most obvious areas to find trout. Other places include gravel bars, inlets and outlets, sunken river beds, and dropoffs. From these places, fish can dart quickly into deep water or weed beds, the chief sheltering areas of the lake.

Finding fish in stream or lake is a matter of understanding why they seek out certain places. With a little careful thought, the angler can greatly narrow the choices and increase his chances for success.

Chapter 5

NYMPHING THE FILM

Nymph fishing started in the film. It was G. E. M. Skues, a fisher of the chalk streams of southern England at the turn of the century, who established nymph fishing as a separate and respected angling strategy. He observed that many of the trout were feeding not on adults, but on nymphs which were drifting just below the surface. Seeing a rising fish, he said, most anglers would hammer it with a dry fly, "being wholly unconscious that for hours and days at a time these trout were feeding on nymphs and were letting the natural hatched-out insect go by." At first he thought the trout were taking nymphs in the act of hatching and used a wet fly as an emerger pattern. But later, he observed unhatched nymphs in the mouths of some trout he had caught and thereafter tied his patterns without wings as strictly nymphal imitations. These were beautifully done flies that stressed the shapes, sizes, and colors of the naturals. In the honored tradition of the chalk streams, he fished only

Figure 5-1. A Skues nymph.

to rising trout, presenting the nymph delicately in or just below the surface. Skues was a master angler, and his *Nymph Fishing for Chalk Stream Trout* is an amazing collection of lucid observations on this subject. The angling lessons offered in that little volume are as germane today as they were revolutionary and inflammatory in those exclusive days of the dry fly.

It has been only recently that fly fishermen have widely recognized the importance of the insect during the act of hatching. Doug Swisher and Carl Richards provided the impetus that has stimulated a rethinking of this aspect of nymph fishing. Their books, *Selective Trout* and *Trout Fishing Strategy*, are a cornucopia of new ways of looking at old ideas. The importance of emergers, stillborns, and dry nymphs in the trout's diet is firmly established in these two volumes; all serious nymph fishers should read them in detail.

These various hatching stages are not important for all aquatic insects. Nearly always, nymphs of stoneflies, dragonflies, damselflies, and the *Isonychia* and *Siphlonurus* mayflies crawl out of the water

Figure 5-2. An *Isonychia* mayfly hatching on a rock.

before transforming to the adult. Pupae of some species of caddises climb out of the water before the adult emerges. Larvae of dobsonflies, fish flies, alderflies, beetles, craneflies, and some midges crawl from the water before pupation. Those insects which transform from the immature to the adult stage while still in the water are most of the mayflies, caddises, and midges.

The emergence process is the same for all insects that transform in the water. The nymphal or pupal case splits between the shoulders and

Figure 5-3. The Giant Michigan Mayfly (*Hexigenia limbata*) emerging in the film.

the adult pops out: wings first, then head and forelegs, then abdomen and hindlegs. The adult must then expand and dry its wings before it can take flight. From the time the case splits until the adult has fully expanded its wings, the insect is called an emerger. Thus, there are emergers in all stages of transformation: nymphs or pupae with rumpled adult wings just emergent, adults half way out of the immature husk, and emergent adults with unexpanded wings.

The process of emergence is not without its nuances. Some individuals transform quite rapidly; others of the same species are more slow to free themselves. Yet others are unable to complete the molt and eventually drown; these were named "stillborns" by Swisher and Richards. The stillborn is a classic Greek monster, caught between immature and adult stages and unable to function in either role. They are adults with the nymphal or pupal case hanging on the aft portion of the abdomen and thus are longer than either immature or adult

Figure 5-4. A stillborn mayfly awash at the film.

insect. All aquatic species that hatch in the water have a proportion of stillborns in the emerging population.

At the beginning of a hatch, many trout will be deep, picking off the insects as they rise from the gravel. As the hatch progresses, the fish will begin to feed heavily at the surface because the film concentrates the insects, which must pause there to complete their molt. This thin zone of dense, relatively inactive organisms is like a smorgasbord to the trout. There are unemerged nymphs or pupae, all stages of emergers, stillborns, and adults floating overhead. Small fish will dash about, grabbing everything in sight. The larger fish, however, must move more body mass and so establish a deliberate rhythm in their feeding. Very often these big trout feed entirely on pupae or nymphs, emergers, and stillborns, never taking an adult. This is more a matter of energy output versus energy gain per unit of time than a matter of personal taste. There are more of these other forms than there are adults; hence, more of these forms can be taken during any one period of time. In addition, it is easier for the fish to establish a feeding rhythm on the copious immature insects than on the scattered adults.

Emergence occurs at or near the surface; however, like all biological phenomena, there are exceptions. Nymphs of the *Epeorus* mayflies (Quill Gordon, for example) are whitewater dwellers. When mature, they line up on the downstream side of submerged rocks; there the adult emerges from the nymphal husk. The emergent adult is no match

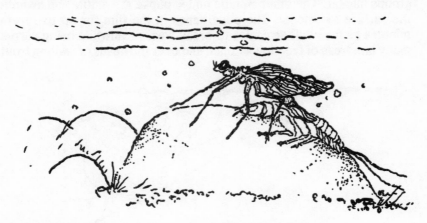

Figure 5-5. A Quill Gordon (*Epeorus pleuralis*) emerging on the bottom.

for the powerful currents and is carried rapidly downstream as it swims toward the surface. At the base of the rapids or in other large, quiet water pockets the adult breaches the surface and sits patiently, waiting for its rumpled wings to enlarge and dry. These are excellent places to nymph the film with an emergent adult pattern.

The other mayflies complete their hatching just below or at the film. The nymph swims to the surface and hangs there while the adult wiggles free. The nymphal husk floats away as the emergent adult sits on the surface to pump up and dry its wings. This process requires one to several minutes. Nymphs, emergers, and stillborns should be fished in the uppermost foot of water.

Caddis pupae are exceptional swimmers, moving quickly from the bottom to the surface. In some species, the adult breaks free of the pupal husk during the rapid ascent. In most instances, however, the pupa halts at the surface, where the adult emerges rather swiftly and takes wing. Pupae, emergers, and stillborns can be fished in the film.

Midges, those small, nonbiting, mosquitolike insects so often seen along streams and lakes, are often supposed by the fly fisher to be too small for trout fodder. But their legion numbers and presence in all waters make them a prime target for foraging fish. Pupae of the net-winged midges, the mountain midges, and the black flies cement them-selves to the bottom, and so the adult must emerge underwater. The mature adult generates gas between itself and the pupal husk. The head of the pupa faces downstream, allowing the adult to emerge in the bubble of gas and pop to the surface in the swift waters that all three groups inhabit. The other aquatic midge pupae are motile and swim to the surface to emerge. The pupa hangs in the film for up to several minutes as the adult struggles to break free, meanwhile being carried many hundreds of feet downstream and over the heads of waiting trout.

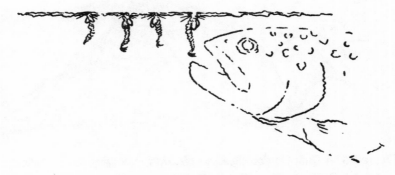

Figure 5-6. Midge pupae hanging in the film during a hatch.

The fish porpoise softly and without hurry, intercepting pupae, emer-gers, and stillborns.

When a fish feeds just below the surface, it often causes the water to hump up or bulge as it rises to intercept the organism then turns downward. Other times the trout may rush to grab the organism then turn away sharply, causing a swirl on the surface. If the insect is on the surface, the fish puts its nose out of the water and flares its gills, vacuuming in the organism. Occasionally the fish will suck the insect off the surface from several inches below; the result is a sudden hole in the water into which the insect has disappeared. Either way, the fish gets air along with his food, and when he turns down, the air is expelled through the gills, leaving a bubble on the surface. Fish bulging or swirling just under the surface will not leave this telltale bubble. Watch for it.

There are times when it is difficult to determine what is being taken. Midges are usually accused of being the culprit when the angler is

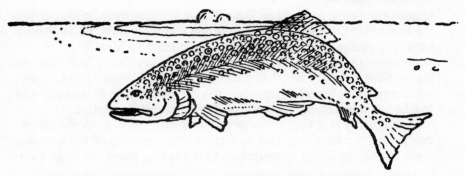

Figure 5-7. Bubbles left by the trout after taking a fly off the surface.

unable to figure out what's hatching. The scenario goes like this: First Angler, "Boy, they were tough today. Fish working all around me and I couldn't get 'em on anything." Second Angler (with an air of authority), "Midges." And it's partially true; midges can be the cause of these perplexing situations. But there are other creatures that can produce equally frustrating hours.

When midges are hatching, there will usually be a cloud of adults hovering and dancing near the surface or along the shoreline. The rise

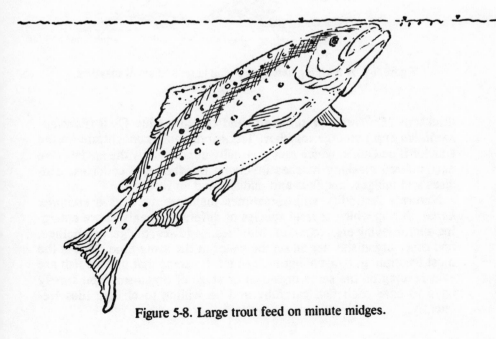

Figure 5-8. Large trout feed on minute midges.

to pupae and emergers will be just a dimple at the surface, often belying the size of the feeding fish. This smutting rise, as it is called, is characteristic of midge hatches. Watch for it and learn to identify it.

The rise to caddises is also unique. The fish chase and bite the fast-moving pupae rather than suck them in. This results in a splashy, sudden rise that leaves *several* bubbles on the surface. If the take was just below the surface, the swirl will often result in a splash.

Occasionally two organisms of different sizes will hatch simultaneously, and the larger species will mask the presence of the smaller. Such a *masking hatch* often occurs in the spring when the large Hen-

Figure 5-9. A masking hatch involving large and small mayflies.

dricksons (*Ephemerella subvaria*) and the tiny Blue Quill (*Paraleptophlebia* spp.) emerge together. Trout frequently concentrate on the smaller Blue Quills, which may go totally unnoticed by the angler. I've encountered masking hatches involving mayflies and caddises, caddises and midges, mayflies and midges, and so forth.

Nature's fecundity will sometimes manifest itself as a *complex hatch*, during which several species of different organisms are emerging and/or laying eggs together. Mayflies, caddises, midges, stoneflies, and other organisms are all on the water at the same time. This is the most frustrating, hair-pulling time of all. It seems that no two fish are ever feeding on the same organism or stage of organism. You simply have to case each fish carefully and be willing to change flies frequently.

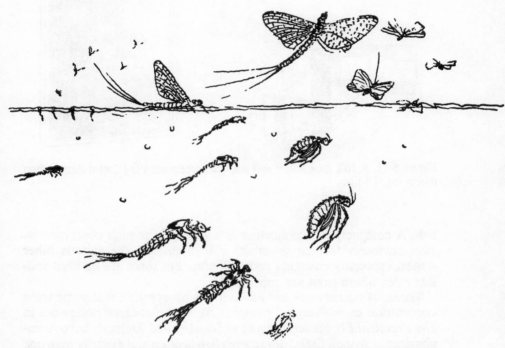

Figure 5-10. A complex hatch of several species of mayflies and caddises.

Once in a while the fish will be feeding at the surface but there will be no hatch. There may be terrestrials in and beneath the film. The rise to terrestrials is often soft, like the smutting rise. Other organisms such as the waterboatman, backswimmer, water beetles, dragonfly and damselfly nymphs, and scuds may be swimming or floating at the film, and fish will be bulging and swirling for them.

With all these possibilities, it would seem that the angler should have a pocket computer to figure his odds before making a cast. Actually, there are three simple steps to untangling this knotty situation. First, observe. Observing is not just looking; it is *seeing*. Invest a few minutes to watch the water and see what's there, the dividends are remarkable. Second, use a surface screen. A simple wire frame, four by five inches, with nylon bridal veil glued on it is quite adequate. Held in the film for several minutes, it will collect any drifting organisms and give an excellent idea of what's being taken. Third, if there are adults on the water, try to get close enough to watch the insects drift over the

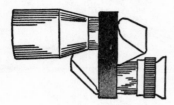

Figure 5-11. A 10X monocular and surface screen are very useful items when nymphing the film.

fish. A compact, 10X monocular is a godsend for such observations. Fish obviously feeding on adults will often take the various other stages, especially emergers and stillborns, but there are no hard-and-fast rules where trout are concerned.

Skues, of course, was not amiss in his observation that some trout concentrate exclusively on nymphs. As A. J. McClane points out in *The Practical Fly Fisherman* and as Swisher and Richards have reemphasized, a nymph fished dry to such fish is often more deadly than one fished under the film. This is especially true of trout nymphing while the hatch is in full swing. Fish the standard nymph pattern, but put floatant on it so it rides right in the film, partially awash. This is a useful tactic to remember.

All emergers and stillborns, regardless of insect order, share a common characteristic. They are a ragtag, rumpled, and disheveled group. The very best imitations are themselves a disreputable-looking lot. There are several successful methods for tying these patterns. A standard nymph can be modified by adding short wings of marabou, rolled nylon hosiery material, polypropylene yarn, and so on. Such a fly imitates the early stages of emergence. Stillborns and partially emergent adults can be fashioned by tying in a tail of ostrich herl, hair, or hackle points to represent the partially cast nymphal or pupal husk; the remainder of the fly is dressed to look like an adult with short, rumpled wings. Emergent adults are tied in this latter fashion but without the husk.

My favorite dressing for the various emerger stages is the Wet/Dry Fly. It's not really a new style of fly, just a twist on the oldest type of fly known—the soft hackled fly. Jim Leisenring was an exceptionally gifted wet fly fisherman and wrote about his love affair with soft hackle patterns in *The Art of Tying the Wet Fly and Fishing the Flymph* (revised by Vernon Hidy). It is a classic study on wet fly angling. Sylvester Nemes's book, *The Soft Hackled Fly*, is entirely devoted to these imitations, but again as wet flies. Actually, the soft hackled fly will float superbly when properly constructed. The soft hackle gives an excellent impression of crumpled wings and legs.

The fly is tied with a dubbed fur body. For the early stages of emergence, body color should match that of the nymph. For later stages, the color should match the body of the adult. The hackle is the key to this fly. The feather should be taken from the shoulder of the wing (covert feather). These coverts have wide yet soft fibers that if dressed with floatant allow the imitation to float in the film; undressed, the fly can be fished wet just beneath the surface.

The cutthroats of the Yellowstone River up in the park have been labeled as easy marks for the fly fisher, but these trout can be frustrat-

Figure 5-12. The Wet/Dry Fly.

ingly selective at times. In the low, clear-water days of August, there is a hatch of size 18 Blue-Winged Olives (*Ephemerella* spp.) during which the fish show surprising sophistication. It is an excellent opportunity to experiment with different patterns.

Fish lying in quiet water pockets watch each natural fly carefully before making a slow and deliberate, complex rise. Fish in faster water drift downstream with the currents and scrutinize each fly before delicately sipping it in and moving back upstream. Not all naturals observed by the fish are taken. When nymphs, nymphs with emerger wings, various styles of emergent adults, and duns were presented to these fish, they selected the Wet/Dry ten to one over all other patterns. I've experienced similar results wherever I've fished the fly: Henry's Fork, Silver Creek, the Brule, Falling Springs, and many other streams. This pattern has earned an honored place in my fly box.

I don't want to make it seem that the Wet/Dry Fly is a panacea for all angling woes. No fly will ever be that good! But it is a very useful fly. It not only works well for the mayflies but also imitates emergers and stillborns of the caddises and midges. In addition, it can be fished dry with action to imitate fluttering duns, caddises, midges, etc., fished wet to simulate dead drifting pupae or emergers, twitched just under the surface to imitate active emergence, fished on the rising swing of the Leisenring Lift, and so forth. The silhouette of this fly is so representative of so many insects that every angler should carry a few of them and give them an honest try. Colors and tying instructions are given in Appendix A.

For the midges, Griffith's Gnat has also proved an effective emerger pattern. Created by George Griffith, one of the founders of Trout Unlimited, these minute flies are nothing but a herl or dubbed body palmered with a tiny grizzly hackle. The halo of hackle gives the impression of a partially cast pupal husk as the fly floats in the film.

Skues cast only to rising fish, and this is still the best way for nymphing the film. When the trout are up working the surface, they can be easily located and presented with the fly. Remember that the best position to place your fly is ahead and to your side of the fish (see chapter 3). The trout will see the fly when it lands on the surface but

Figure 5-13. Place the fly upstream and to your side of the fish.

not be spooked by the leader and line. If the fly is floating, the fish will not see it clearly until it reaches the edge of his window. He will simply wait for the fly to come to him. If the fly sinks, the trout will see it in its entirety as soon as it punctures the film. In this instance the fish may quickly rush forward and grab the fly. You must be alert for such a move.

For nymphing just under the surface, the *greased leader* tactic is invaluable. It's true that you sometimes see the fish flash when it intercepts the nymph, or the water may bulge, or you may see the fish open and close its mouth (Skues's "wink underwater"), but often these clues are missing. Grease the leader with a paste-type floatant (I prefer Gink, Fly Cream, or Muclin) to within six inches or so of the fly. Be especially careful not to get any on the fly. The imitation will sink, but the buoyant leader will hold it just under the surface. When a trout intercepts the fly, the leader will draw under sharply; in smooth currents this is very noticeable. This is the tactic that Skues preferred. In choppy currents the leader may be nearly impossible to see. Here, a strike indicator (see chapter 11) will greatly increase your ability to detect strikes.

For some reason, I always associate this tactic with midges, even though it's very useful for any fly. I guess it's because I first learned the tactic for midge fishing. It's absolutely captivating to cast the tiny imitation, see the leader draw under, and tighten on a fish. To me it's the closest thing to magic I've ever experienced; maybe that's the real fascination of this technique.

If the fish are obviously taking flies at the surface, then fish the pupa, nymph, emerger, or stillborn dry. Dress it with a paste-type floatant so it rides right on the surface, partially awash. Strike detection is always difficult when fishing flies down flush in the film. To help see the take, I grease the leader right out to the fly. This also helps make a smooth pickup. When the cast settles to the water, look out along the line and you'll see the surface impression of the floating leader. The distal end of this impression is the general location of the fly. If a fish rises anywhere near it, lift gently. If no hookup occurs, the fly can be allowed to continue in the drift. Sometimes you miss seeing the actual rise, especially in choppy water. Try to watch the leader impression; it can serve as a strike indicator.

The fly can be presented from any angle when fishing the film: upstream, downstream, or across stream. Try to position yourself in such a way that you can get the longest drag-free float and yet be as close as possible to the fish. Be especially alert for drag. Most anglers are very watchful for drag when fishing dry, but few think of it when fishing beneath the surface. If the naturals are drifting in the current and your fly is dragging, it will not be accepted, either on the surface or below. If drag is a problem and you can't correct it by casting or mending tactics, lengthen the tippet and drop it down a size or two in diameter. The thinner, longer tippet will allow a more natural movement of the fly.

George Harvey of State College, Pennsylvania, is an exceptionally skillful fly tier and angler. To fish the low, clear waters of late summer, he prefers a leader composed in large part of small-diameter segments and having a long tippet. Such a leader will not entirely straighten when cast and falls in loose bends on the water. These bends compensate for the confused cross currents encountered in pocket water and spring creek flows. The current must pull all the bends out of the leader before drag occurs; often this period of drag-free float is enough to get a strike.

Case each situation carefully and decide on the best casting tactic to keep all unnecessary slack out of the line. If the rise is directly up-stream, reach the cast to one side so as not to drop the line over the fish. Or, you may have to mend in the air on an upstream cast to get the best line of float without inducing drag. Take up slack created as the line drifts toward you by lifting the rod and stripping line under your finger. When the cast is to be made across stream, reach the line upstream and mend only as necessary for the maximum drag-free float. The reach eliminates initial slack; as the line comes down, tip the rod back to the vertical, following the line's speed on the water. A downstream approach requires the parachute cast; it produces no slack.

Hooking the fish should be done simply by *lifting* the rod tip to tighten the line. Don't strike too quickly. More anglers strike too fast than too slow and pull the fly out of the trout's mouth. Hesitate a second to give the fish a chance to close his mouth. This may sound like heresy, but the fish is sucking in a morsel he obviously believes to be food. He *must* close his mouth on the fly and taste and feel it before he can decide if it's real. Then the fish must open his mouth and spit it out if he decides it isn't edible. This is a matter of seconds, not an instant's doing. I've had trout take the Wet/Dry Fly, for instance, and pull several feet of leader under before the resistance of the line caused the fish to hook itself.

Keeping slack out of the line is essential for detecting strikes, but it is also necessary for properly hooking the fish. If slack has been kept to a minimum, the hookup will be immediate. You will be in position to make a *controlled* strike. If there's excess slack in the line when the fish takes the fly, however, the tendency is to strike too hard, trying desperately to pull out the slack with a power stroke that neatly parts the leader.

The upstream approach can produce a difficult strike situation. Raising the rod tip to take up slack will eventually bring the rod back to the vertical. This is an awkward moment to have the fish take your fly. You can't make a gentle lift of the rod tip; there's no more lift left. But there are a couple of ways to overcome this troublesome problem. First, don't lift the rod entirely to the vertical. Take up slack solely by stripping in line; when the rise occurs, simply lift the rod tip. If you do get the rod back to the vertical and a strike occurs, snap the rod *forward and down*, just as though making a roll cast. The line will tighten when the roll forms and pull the hook home.

From downstream or across stream, you pull the fly back into the corner of the trout's mouth. However, when fishing downstream, you are pulling the fly straight forward and out of the fish's mouth. Hooking a fish on the downstream parachute cast requires an iron will. You really have to hesitate. After the fish rises, say to yourself, "Now I have you"; then pull the hook home. When you can hook nine out of ten fish on the downstream approach, consider yourself an accomplished angler!

Nymphing the film was first, and it's still an exciting and deadly way to take trout. Many times I've fished the entire hatch in this way. Nymphs first, as the hatch started, then Wet/Dry Fly emergers and stillborns, stalking individual fish in the time-honored manner of Skues.

Chapter 6

STRIP/TEASE NYMPH FISHING

The March 1961 issue of *Sports Afield* carried an article by Ernie Schwiebert entitled "Early-Season Trout Secrets." In addition to the beautifully drawn flies there was expert advice on tactics with a sinking line. Try as I might, I could not locate one, but Christmas brought fulfillment of the coveted dream, and a new sinking fly line was wound on an extra reel spool in readiness. Trout season opened in mid-April, and the icy chill of winter was still evident in the shadow of Tussey Mountain. The crystalline water of Laurel Run spilled over the dam, ducked under the little fieldstone bridge, and wound its way through the tangle of evergreen shrubs.

Trout were there, too, plainly visible in the tail of the bridge pool, and they were working. But their activity was confined to the coarse rubble of the bottom; finning gently in the quiet bottom currents, they would dart forward, then slowly drift back, or twist sharply and poke their noses into the rocks, flashing their silvery sides. As I watched, I suddenly realized what I was seeing. "Nymphing, they're taking dis-

Figure 6-1. Nymphing fish.

lodged naturals or rooting them out!" It was a thought that quickened the pulse of imagination.

Where the currents struck the stone abutment, they turned under, pulling the line and leader quickly to the bottom. "Fish slow and deep," Schwiebert's article had said, "using the hand twist retrieve." Other authors had mentioned an occasional strip of the line. I moved the stonefly nymph slowly, stopped it and let the fly bounce back downstream a short ways, then started with a strip. The strong pull of a fifteen-inch rainbow was unexpected on the first cast, but the fish was firmly hooked and eventually brought to net. A number of other trout, only slightly smaller, were taken on subsequent casts. These were trophy trout for this stream, and the ease of their capture confirmed the use of the sinking line and this stop-start retrieve. Ten years later, Ed Mueller of Indianapolis, Indiana, and I were discussing this tactic, and he said he called it the "*strip/tease*." The name is most appropriate.

Some nymphs crawl about, some swim weakly, some are powerful swimmers, but all move in shuttlelike fashion—scurrying, pausing, scurrying, pausing—moving from one piece of cover to the next, never staying exposed long. Caught in a current, they tumble along until they can secure a foothold. The strip/tease technique allows the angler to imitate these basic patterns of movement. The slow hand-twist retrieve mimics the crawling or slow swimming pattern, the occasional pause punctuates the motion in the same way the natural does, and the quick strip apes the darting action. In the stream, releasing a little line allows the fly to bounce along like a dislodged natural.

The strip/tease can be used with a sinking line in a variety of stream situations. Pools are most obvious. In the pool proper the quiet water allows the line time to get down and allows it to stay down while the fly is worked back. Normally the fly is cast up and across to give it plenty of time to sink. *Don't rush!* The most important thing you need for this approach is patience. Count to sixty; more if the pool is very deep. While the line is sinking, lower your rod tip until it's only a couple of feet off the water and keep it pointed directly down the line. Be sure you have the line under the index finger of your rod hand so you'll have instant control. Sometimes the fish intercept the nymph as it sinks. With the rod tip low and the line under your finger, you'll be able to feel the take.

When the line is on the bottom, begin the retrieve. First, use the hand twist to gather the line *slowly*. Remember to always pull the line across the index finger of your rod hand. After you move the nymph a foot or so, stop. Count to ten; then start the slow retrieve again. After a few repeats of the slow crawl/stop motion, give the line a sudden strip

or two and stop. Start with the slow crawl again and repeat the process
Trout intercept the fly at any time; so remain alert. If, when you begin
the retrieve after a pause, the line feels heavy or tight, a fish could have
your fly. Keeping the line across your index finger will increase your
ability to detect this soft pickup. Often the fish will take the fly solidly
and there's no mistaking the strike.

Try varying the retrieve by omitting the strip; simply crawl the fly
slowly, let it stop, crawl it again, and so forth. This was Ray Bergman's
favorite nymphing retrieve. Hewitt mentions in *A Trout and Salmon
Fisherman for 75 Years* that the speed of the retrieve should be slow
and even; if the fly suddenly speeds up, the fish will reject it. I have seen
this, especially when a fish is following the fly in the upper layers of
water, but I've also had plenty of trout take the fly hard when I gave it a
sudden strip. Don't get locked in on one tactic and forget that ex-
perimentation is a big part of angling.

Where riffles shelve off into a pool, the strip/tease can be most
effectively used. Anglers on the White River in Missouri and Arkansas
work scud imitations in such places during periods of low water flow
from the dams. They stand well back from the lip and cast their heavily
weighted imitations out into the deep water and permit them to sink.
Shot is often added to the leader to keep the fly right on the bottom.
The nymph is then slowly drawn up over the dropoff. This tactic regu-
larly accounts for huge rainbows—many over ten pounds!

The confluence of two currents below an island or other obstruction
often produces downwelling water. You can recognize the confluence
line where the currents mix because the surface is all choppy. Such a
place will rapidly pull the line to the bottom and hold it there as the
angler fishes the fly directly back upstream by the strip/tease method.
Fishing the strip/tease at the edge of the main current tongue where it
enters a pool also requires a straight downstream or upstream cast and
shot on the leader.

The plunge pool beneath a dam or waterfall is an excellent place to
take trout with this nymphing tactic. The sinking line is presented
parallel to the dam and into the falling water. The cast will be carried
rapidly to the bottom, where the fly is then worked along in the deepest
part of the pool. On one of the streams I fished when I was in high
school there are a couple of small dams. One is at a pump house, the
other is caused by the foundation of a railroad trestle. During a trip
home, I decided to fish the stream. The *Isonychia* mayflies were active,
and the Red Brown Nymph proved deadly. At the pump house, there
were no fish showing in the tail of the pool; so I cut into the woods and
came out next to the dam. Using a bush for cover, I pitched the sinking

Figure 6-2. Cast parallel to the falls to reach the prime lie under the falling water.

line out into the falling water and let it settle for a full minute. The fly had only been retrieved two inches when I felt a soft tap. It was a beautifully marked fifteen-inch brown that fought deep and strong, thoroughly spooking the pool.

I released him and headed cross country for the trestle pool. There were a couple of big browns in that pool and it seemed as though this was going to be the morning. The line hadn't fully settled when I felt the tap. I pulled the hook home and felt a heavy surge from deep in the pool, but as I backed it down, I suddenly realized the fish was smaller than I had thought. It was still a trophy though; a deep crimson belly showed, and I landed a foot-long chub.

A mile above my parents' house, there's a small brook trout stream that I often fished. It emerges from a thickly wooded valley and flows through a neighbor's pastures and hay fields. Terrestrial patterns were often successful there, but the best trout fell to nymphs and the strip/tease. The fly was cast downstream and placed so that it would sink and be carried back under an overhanging bank, log, or cress bed. The nymph was worked back upstream to the outer edge of the pocket, then permitted to drift back into the depths again. Often a trout would slam

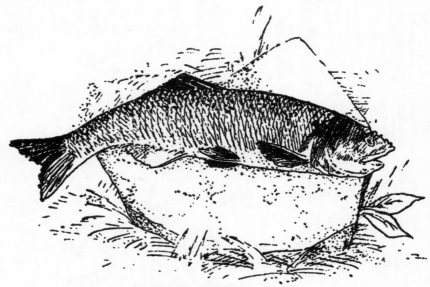

Figure 6-3. A trophy horned chub.

the fly on the first retrieve, but sometimes several minutes would pass before the tactic was too tempting for the trout, and it would rush forward and seize the fly with a savage strike. Twelve- and thirteen-inch brooks, several fine browns, and the first naturally reproduced tiger trout I ever caught came from that little stream, victims of the strip/tease.

Lakes are ideal for this stop-start nymphing tactic. During the bright part of the day, fish usually lie deep along rocky points, sunken logs, old creek beds, and dropoffs. Beds of vegetation also provide shelter; fish may lie in pockets in the weeds, hold just in the uppermost layers of the weeds (whether deep or shallow), or cruise the deep water side of the bed where the weeds form a dropoff. The sunken line is useful for all these places.

The best way to fish near the bottom is the countdown method described by Schwiebert in *Nymphs*. Cast the line and count until it reaches the bottom. The line will often go slack when it gets completely down. On subsequent casts, count the line down to within a count or two of the bottom; then begin the retrieve. This will prevent snags but still keep the line close to the bottom. The sink rate will depend on the density of the line you use. A sinking line comparable to the Wet Cel II by Scientific Anglers is fine. Deep water can more easily be fished with a denser line, but you run into the problem of the line continuing to sink as it's retrieved and the fly getting hung up. The floating-tip, sinking line described in chapter 1 is the best bet for this situation. The line can go down fast, but the fly will still be held up off the bottom.

Remember that the line is not out on the surface; it bows deeply to the bottom. This shortens the effective length of the cast; for example, a forty-foot cast in twenty feet of water will only give you about twenty feet of effective fishing. If the trout are on the bottom and there's no concern about a take as the fly sinks, make the cast and then dump a

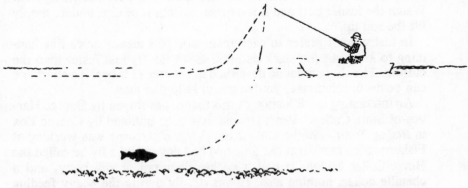

Figure 6-4. The effective fishing length of a sinking line is much less than the length of the cast.

bunch of line on the water right at the rod tip. This extra line will sink and form the deep bow in the line; thus, the effective length of the cast will not be shortened.

For nymphing deep in fast water, I use a short leader, but in lakes and slow pools I use the 100-inch leader, often with a 30-inch tippet. First, there aren't any strong bottom upwellings to push the line and leader toward the surface. Second, fish in quiet waters often follow the fly for some distance before they take it, and I don't want the line to spook them.

The use of this tactic is not restricted to a sinking line; when the fish are shallow, a floating line is used. In streams the best time to use the shallow strip/tease is during a hatch. The nymphs will be swimming to the surface and can easily be mimicked by this tactic. Edward Hewitt, who was America's first really great nymph fisher, strongly recommended long, fine leaders when using this tactic: "Long as well as fine leaders are an absolute necessity for nymph fly fishing." He recommended leaders of 10 to 15 feet tapered to .007-inch gut or smaller. This was fine tackle in those days. I use a 150-inch leader or a 100-incher with a 3- or 4-foot tippet. If the fish are feeding just under the surface, grease the leader butt with a paste-type fly floatant so it rides high on the film. This will not only keep the fly high in the water, but it will enable you to see the take much better.

In pools, the fly may be presented upstream, across stream or downstream, whichever way you can get the best presentation. I prefer to make a straight cast and drop the rod tip as the line comes down, ending with the tip a couple of feet above the water and pointing directly down the line. The fly is then retrieved past the rising fish. Watch the leader butt and if it pauses, twitches, or dips under, simply lift the rod tip.

In fast water I prefer to cast upstream. This means quick line handling to keep out the slack and still move the fly just faster than the current. The shotgun tactic described in chapter 11 is best if a short line can be used; otherwise, you've got to strip like mad.

An interesting modification of this tactic, developed by George Harvey of State College, Pennsylvania, has been outlined by Charlie Fox in *Rising Trout*. Charlie calls it the *fast rod*. George was working at Fisherman's Paradise at the time and had developed a fly he called the Horse-Collar Midge. It had a hackle fiber tail, a silk body, and a chenille collar, nothing else. It was deadly during the heavy feeding

Figure 6-5. George Harvey's Horse-Collar Midge.

activity among the midge hatches that occurred at dusk. The technique was to cast the fly down and across a broken water run and let it swing into the quiet water just at the edge of the current. When the fly entered the edge, the rod tip was held high and the fly jiggled, moving it around in the quiet water. The pattern and technique were so effective that George usually had a gallery watching him fish.

On lakes, in the evening and early morning, on overcast days, and during a hatch, the trout are up near the surface or cruising near the shoreline. Under these conditions, a floating line is a necessity. If the fish are inshore, then you must be very careful when approaching them. One method is to stay well back from the edge and cast across the land. In these situations the fish are often visible and the wingshooting and jumping nymph tactics are extremely effective (see chapter 9). These methods are no problem if the bank is grassy or sandy, but if there's high bushes or cattails, then the best approach is from the water. If you use a boat, keep it well out away from shore—at least fifty feet. This will mean some long casts, but if you insist on getting closer, you'll spook more fish than you catch. Another route open to you is to use a belly boat. With this inner tube device you can get closer to the fish than you can in a boat because you're lower in the water and can move silently. I prefer an eight and one-half or nine-foot

Figure 6-6. A belly boat allows a quiet, close approach in lakes.

rod for a four- or five-weight line when I fish out of either a boat or a belly boat. The longer rod helps keep the line up during the casting stroke, and the light line is not so apt to spook the fish.

I fished with such a rod and line one April when a strong east wind added bite to the cool air. As my party unfastened the boat from its moorings, I noticed a large number of waterboatmen in the shallows and suggested we head across to a sheltered cove. We stayed well out from shore and began a methodical probing with our flies, casting as close to the bank as possible—sometimes right up onto the sand—and working the fly back with the strip/tease. Fish usually intercepted the fly within five feet of the shoreline, and the take was often very delicate. But, by greasing the leader all the way out to the tippet, we could see the leader twitch as the trout mouthed the fly. With the rod tip low and pointing directly down the straight line, only a gentle lift of the rod was necessary and the fish was on. The fishes' mouths often contained waterboatmen. It was an exciting afternoon, rich with lessons in the subtleties of the strip/tease.

In lakes there are often submerged weedbeds that rise close to the surface; the trout will cruise above the weeds watching for organisms in the upper parts of the plants. A nymph strip/teased through these

Figure 6-7. Trout cruise over weeds watching for food organisms.

areas is often quite effective. Another favorite cruising lane for trout is along the outer edge of the weedbed where it suddenly drops off into the deep water of the lake. The fish move along the edge of the bed, usually several feet below the tops of the plants, and watch for food organisms. The deep water and the weedbed offer instant protection. Anchor the boat twenty to twenty-five feet back from the outer edge of the bed and cast the nymph about twenty feet beyond the weeds. Use a weighted fly and don't grease the leader; you want the fly to get down five to ten feet. Keep the rod tip low and pointing straight down the line. Work the fly back with a slow strip/tease. The fish usually pick up the fly as it nears the edge. Often they simply stop the fly or suck it in during the pause. Watch the tip of the line for any unusual movement and be sensitive to any difference in the feel of the line as you begin the movement after the pause. If the line feels tight or offers resistance, lift the rod tip.

While I normally fish the strip/tease in a slow, deliberate fashion, there are times when a fast-moving fly is most productive. One summer

I encountered a massive shoreward migration of damselfly nymphs as they prepared to hatch. Trout were cruising over a weedbed, swirling and slashing at the swimming insects. A slow-moving fly took a few trout, but when the retrieve was speeded up until the fly was literally zipping through the water, strikes came on every cast. The trout would rush twenty or thirty feet and grab the fly. It was totally unnerving. Often the bulges and swirls made by the fish as they dashed for the fly would cause me to strike too soon. I then watched the greased leader butt; when a fish took the nymph, the leader would jump sharply and the strike would be positive. A faster retrieve can also be used to imitate the motion of dragonfly nymphs and the fast-swimming mayflies, but remember, most people fish this retrieve too fast rather than too slow.

This method is a basic tactic in my arsenal of nymphing techniques since it requires no special equipment and is applicable to a wide range of angling situations. Trout are suckers for the strip/tease.

Chapter 7

OLD STANDBY

When I think of cutthroat trout, it is always with visions of buck-skinned men, shining mountains, and majestic rivers. The cutthroat is my time machine that transports me to the primal places of boyhood dreams, and nowhere is this lure of *Salmo clarki* stronger than in Yellowstone Park. To me this restless land of fumaroles, mudpots, and geysers is the finest cutthroat fishery on earth. Outflow from the lake

Figure 7-1. The bubbling, hissing land of Yellowstone Park.

forms the mighty Yellowstone River, which courses northward 671 miles to its confluence with the Missouri. Cutthroats, spawned in the upper reaches of the river, grow large on the abundant insects and crustaceans.

One day with currents tugging at my waders, I eased closer to fish rising over an algae bed in midriver. I put the cast just above them. A brightly colored cockfish of about two pounds took the scud as it swung across the current only a foot under the surface. The trout took advantage of the heavy pull of the river and the long line, fighting deep and strong. When the fish was close, I caught the fly and backed out the barbless hook. A large trout showed about thirty feet out, and I caught my breath as his broad tail slid beneath the surface. The fly drifted over his position and several feet beyond. As the line pulled out of the water on the backcast, the fish took the fly. The leader broke under the sudden stress, and I false-cast violently several times, disgusted at my haste and indiscretion. Suddenly my anger was gone and I felt silly. The trout continued to feed heavily, and in that hour, before darkness and the cold of the river forced me to shore, twenty-six fish between one and three pounds were landed and released.

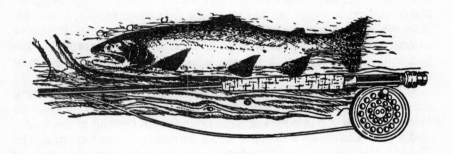

Figure 7-2. A cutthroat from the Yellowstone River.

The down-and-across tactic was the first style of wet fly angling. It's the *old standby* that has served numerous generations of fly fishers: from Dame Juliana Berners to the famous salmon fisher Arthur H. E. Woods to the notable Edward Hewitt to contemporary anglers such as Schwiebert, Whitlock, and Swisher.

The basic method of the down-and-across approach is uncomplicated. The angler fishes downstream, and the fly is cast down and across, then allowed to swing in the current to the angler's side of the stream. This simple method is the one I used on the Yellowstone. The rod tip is kept up and follows the line. Because the current holds the line continuously taut, the take is always positive, with the fish usually hooking itself. If it's a big trout, the leader may not be able to withstand the combined force of the hit and the current pressure on the line.

Schwiebert mentions the old wet fly angler's trick of keeping a foot or so of extra line between your index finger and the reel. When the fish strikes, release that foot of line to ease the sheer stress on the tippet. It's good advice.

Charlie Fox describes this down-and-across approach for use with a wet ant fished in slow waters. Bob McCafferty tied a size 14, hard-bodied black ant that he fished slowly and carefully, casting across or down and across to likely holding lies and allowing the current to slowly draw the fly away. Other ant patterns followed as did other colors and sizes, but the *slow draw* remained; it was the key to success. Small Muskrat Nymphs, Wooly Worms, Scuds, Wet/Dry Flies, and so on are quite effective when fished in this manner. The slow draw has become one of my favorite tactics for nymphing on spring creeks.

I also like this simple approach in briskly moving stretches like riffles and runs for imitations that represent active organisms such as scuds, dragonfly nymphs, caddis pupae, and the swimming mayfly nymphs. It's often best to jiggle the rod tip as the fly swings across; however, with the rod tip moving it's hard to detect a subtle take. If you're casting to a fish, watch for a bulge or flash as the fly approaches his position; otherwise, watch for the leader or line to pause or draw under.

This animated version of the down-and-across swing is potent during the hatching or ovipositing activities of the caddisflies. For these lively insects, I often use two flies, a pupa imitation on the end of the leader and a Poly-Caddis on a dropper about 24 inches above the pupa. The Poly-Caddis is a dry fly tied with a dubbed fur body, a hackle palmered over the thorax and trimmed top and bottom, and a polypropylene yarn wing tied downwing style. It floats like a cork. The Poly-Caddis is riffle-hitched (Fig. 7-3) so that it will side-slip in the current as the cast swings. I like to fish this setup right where a riffle dumps into a pool.

Figure 7-3. Riffle-hitching a fly.

Standing above the pool, cast down and across the water. If you stand in midstream, the fly can be worked back and forth across the currents by moving the rod from one side to the other. I've had good trout leap and cavort about like fingerlings as they slash and grab at the dancing flies. It's a most exciting way to pull up a trout.

Large rivers are always intimidating. Their ponderous volumes and vast expanses leave the angler in a state of frustrated indecision about where to start first. A research report of the Montana Fish and Game Commission solved this problem for me. Electrofishing the Madison, Yellowstone, Big Hole, and other rivers for a survey study, they discovered that 80 to 90 percent of the fish were within thirty feet of the shore, many within ten feet. The reason for this bank hugging is simple: the water is slower and more food organisms are found next to shore. I wade out to fish gravel bars downstream from islands, beds of vegetation, or pockets in shallow riffles; otherwise, I fish big rivers as if they were two thirty-foot-wide streams, one flowing along each side of the channel.

The old standby is a good way to cover the shoreward water. On the big Rocky Mountain rivers, the fly of choice is a heavily weighted Mono Stonefly Nymph. These insects are the most abundant invertebrate form in these large rivers, and they're present year-round. The great size of many stonefly nymphs makes them a prized morsel for even the largest trout. The line I choose depends upon water depth. If the inshore depth is only a few feet, I use a floating line. Gink, Fly Cream, or Muclin is applied to the line to keep it high, but the leader should sink. The angler stands on shore and casts up and across, then simply allows the fly to float free as the rod follows it down. Keep the rod tip up. This free-float period gives the fly a chance to sink. Watch the line/leader junction for any sign of a pause, twitch, or irregular movement that could indicate a take. When the line comes tight in the currents, allow it to swing down and across to your side (Fig. 7-4). Be ready! Many strikes come at the point where the line begins to slide across the current. At that point, the nymph, which was tumbling along the bottom, suddenly gains orientation, and not only begins to move down and across, but rises to the surface. A trout rarely passes up the chance to sock a nymph that jumps up in front of his nose. When the fly is hanging directly downstream, jiggle it around for a few moments using the fast rod technique; then work it back upstream for several feet with the strip/tease. Lift the line as quietly as possible, take one step downstream, and repeat the cast. In this fashion, you can cover a large amount of water during a day's angling.

If you spot a particularly good-looking lie, time the cast so that the

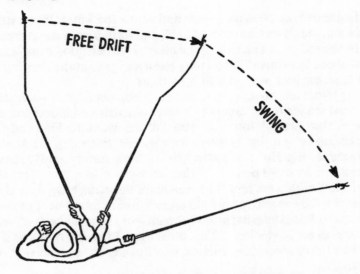

Figure 7-4. Covering shoreward water with the old standby.

fly arrives at that spot just as the line comes tight in the current. The nymph will tumble down into the lie and then jump up off the bottom and swing out of the lie. You can make the fly pause in the lie by releasing line just as the fly reaches that critical point. The extra line sliding out through the guides retards the start of the cross-current swing.

If the water is more than a couple of feet deep, use a sinking line to get the fly down and keep it down as it drifts into the swing. Be sure to follow the line with the rod and keep the tip up to absorb the shock of a strike. During the drift you can't watch the line/leader junction, but the pressure of the water on the sunken line usually keeps it tight enough so you can feel a take.

A unique variation on the down-and-across was developed in the early years of this century by Arthur H. E. Woods. On the big salmon rivers he fished, the current was often spread over a large area so that there was no readily definable current tongue, but the water at the center or at one side still flowed faster than the rest of the water. He used a greased floating line, but a sinking tip line can also be used. The fly is placed across and slightly up. When the fastest flow is in the center, the line is mended upstream whenever it begins to bow in the middle. If the current is fastest where the fly is placed, the mends have to be made downstream to eliminate the bows. The mends *drift* the fly across the current; without them, the line would come tight and *swing* the fly across. The drifting fly lies crossways to the current and presents a side view to the fish. It was Woods's contention that a salmon was more apt to rise to the fly when he got a good side view of it. Between 1913 and 1934 he took 3,490 salmon from his favored Scottish rivers with this method. Proof enough! This *greased line* tactic is now a standard among Atlantic salmon fishermen.

Joe Brooks was thoroughly versed in this tactic and adapted it for streamer fishing on his beloved western rivers. It was a smashing success for big browns. Sylvester Nemes writes about the greased line for fishing the traditional Scottish, soft hackle flies. His arguments for the fly and the method are compelling.

Where there are definite current tongues, you want to drift the fly along their edges. If there's a strong central current, cast to your side first, reaching the cast up and across. Lift the rod as the line comes down to keep as much of it as possible off the slow water between you and the current edge. Lead the fly slightly with the rod tip; that is, keep the rod tip moving downstream just ahead of the line. On a small stream, you can simply hold the line up off the slow water; but on a big river where this isn't possible, an upstream bow will develop, and you'll have to mend the line *downstream*. Try to keep the fly right at the current edge. When the fly is down and across from you, pull it into the slow water with a smooth, slow motion of the rod (Fig. 7-5). This

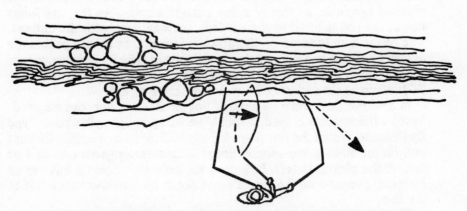

Figure 7-5. Mending downstream to drift the fly at the near edge of fast water.

tactic also works when there is a strong current against the far bank.

To fish the far edge of a strong central current, reach the cast up and across and lift the rod as the line comes down. Again, if the stream is small, just hold the line up off the current. On large streams, a bow will develop downstream and you'll have to mend *upstream*. When the fly is down and across from you, it will begin to swing across the current. Mend as often as necessary to keep the line from bowing downstream. The fly will move diagonally down and across (Fig. 7-6). This tactic also works when the fast water is next to your bank.

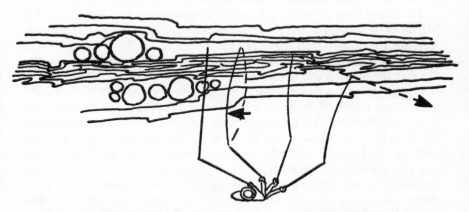

Figure 7-6. Mending upstream to drift the fly at the far edge of fast water.

In a riffle or a flat where current speed is quite uniform, the cast is reached upstream so that it drops straight across. As the line floats down, the rod is lifted to the vertical, keeping pace with the current. The rod is then lowered on the downstream side as the fly passes the angler's position and the line slowly stripped in. The fly is drawn across the current as it drifts down, moving diagonally across the stream (Fig. 7-7), whereas the swinging fly would describe an arc.

In uniform flow either a sinking line or floating line can be used. When a floating line is used, it should be well greased with a paste-type fly floatant. Watch the line point for any indication of a strike. Current pull on the sinking line usually keeps it tight enough so a take can be felt. If the pickup is soft, however, the only signal you'll have is an increasing tension on the line. You've got to be sensitive to the feel of the line.

These drifting techniques sound complicated, and, granted, they're more difficult than casting a straight line and letting it swing, but they are excellent for presenting imitations of nymphs that aren't normally very active swimmers. Stonefly nymphs, many mayfly nymphs and emergers, and wooly worm larvae are well fished with this drift.

Alfred Miller ("Sparse Gray Hackle") in his delightfully witty book, *Fishless Days, Angling Nights*, says that the "greatest lure" of night

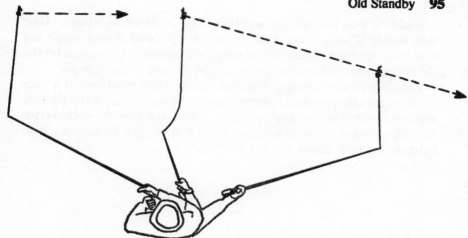

Figure 7-7. Drifting the fly in uniformly flowing water.

fishing is the sheer terror of it. And there's a great deal of truth to this statement. The mind populates the dark with all manner of frightening creatures that lurk at the conscious edge of thought, ready to spring into being with the first unidentified night noise. Russ Wiskowski was returning from fishing one of our favorite night pools when his flashlight failed. He was alone and in a particularly gloomy section of the forest where big hemlocks overhung the trail. Fog crept through the area, adding to the forbidding and lonely feeling. Just as Russ gingerly entered the deepest part of this pitch-black hole, an owl screeched from a limb directly over his head. He said it took two bottles of Vitalis to get his hair back down.

Big browns often feed at dusk and after dark. Night fishing for these large trout is very effective, and the old standby is a basic approach. In *Night Fishing for Trout,* Jim Bashline says, "This business of giving the fish the right 'look' at the fly is the foundation . . . of night fishing . . . a good salmon fisherman should make a great night fisherman, and vice versa." The idea is to *drift* the wet fly into the trout's position. At night, big trout are slow and deliberate in their rise, and the fly must come to them in a slow and deliberate fashion.

In the dusk and dark, trout forage in the tails of pools, the shallows next to a sudden dropoff, the heads of runs, gravel bars in riffles, the edges of pools, and the base of riffles where they fan out into the pool. All these areas should be fished *quietly* and *carefully*. Obviously you should know the water and be well versed in the tactics you plan to use. Daytime scouting is strongly recommended.

Bashline uses big, winged wet flies, but the Muskrat Nymph, Hair Leg Wooly Worm, Scud, Red Brown Nymph, and Strip Nymph are excellent night flies when drifted down and across. I sometimes let the fly swing rather than drift; this is a good method in quiet pools.

The riffle hitch is another modification Bashline mentions. It's very good where there is some current, since the hitch makes the fly ride sideways to the flow on a swinging line. When you hear the sucking rise of a big brown as it slurps up your riffled nymph, you'll become a firm believer in night fishing and the old standby.

Chapter 8

CADDIS MANIA

Caddis flies are unique, if only because they are so numerous in our trout streams. In *The Caddis Flies or Trichoptera of Illinois*, Herbert H. Ross says that the Hydropsychidae caddises are "the most abundant faunal element in most of the rivers and streams" in the Midwest. And that's only *one family* within the vastly larger order to which all caddises belong. Caddises are also very abundant in the East and West. There can be little doubt that these insects are important in the diet of the trout.

Caddises have a complete life cycle like the butterflies and moths: there is a larva (caterpillar), pupa, and adult. The larva and pupa of the caddis fly are aquatic; the adult is terrestrial. Most species have a one-year life cycle, but frequently there are overlapping generations so that adults of some species are coming off all summer long.

The larva is wormlike in appearance and soft-bodied. The abdomen is strongly segmented, and the legs are short. Many species of larvae construct cases of pebbles, sticks, leaves, sand grains, or other bottom trash, gluing the pieces together with silk secreted from special glands near their mouths. Many of the various families, genera, and even species of case builders produce structures unique unto themselves. Through careful observation, cases become as definitive as fingerprints (see Appendix B).

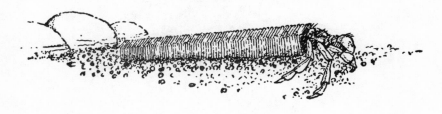

Figure 8-1. *Brachycentrus* caddis larva in case.

The case may be cemented to the bottom or dragged around wher ever the larva travels, and serves as protection against other insect predators. Trout ingest case and all, their powerful stomach juices digesting the larva and the silk bindings of the case. The pebbles and twigs often found in the trout's stomach are not mistakes, they're the remains of caddis cases. Tying and fishing the cased caddis larvae is difficult, though some patterns using the case of the natural as a covering over a yarn core have been locally successful.

Some caddis larvae build a permanent home and erect a net that strains the currents for food. The larva emerges periodically from its

Figure 8-2. Nets of Hydropsychidae caddises.

house and crawls about over the net scraping off any food trapped there. These are the Hydropsychidae caddises. The larvae of all Hydropsychidae caddises are extremely uniform in appearance and habits. They have bushy abdominal gills and prefer riffles, fast runs,

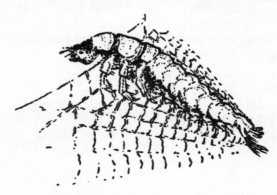

Figure 8-3. Hydropsychidae larva on net.

rapids, and other swift water areas. Occasionally they lose their footing and are swept into the currents. Trout watch for them on the nets and drifting in the currents. These are the most important caddis larvae to the fly fishers of the East and Midwest.

The Green Rock Worm (*Rhyacophila* spp.) is a totally free spirit. These emerald beauties roam about, building neither homes nor nets. They are predaceous, feeding on midges and other small life forms.

Figure 8-4. Green Rock Worm (*Rhyacophila* spp.)

These larvae lack abdominal gills and are found in swiftly flowing, clean water streams. Good populations occur in the East and Midwest, but the western United States is especially blessed with these insects.

Imitations of these noncased Hydropsychidae and Green Rock Worm larvae should stress the strong segmentation of the abdomen, the dark thorax, short legs, and colors of the naturals. The Hydropsychidae patterns should also show pronounced abdominal gilling. There are several methods of tying larval imitations which are most adequately described in Larry Solomon and Eric Leiser's fine book *The Caddis and the Angler*. It is the first really definitive text exclusively aimed at the caddises; it is a necessary addition to the serious fly fisher's collection. The patterns I prefer are given in Appendix A.

Caddis larvae are bottom-dwelling organisms that do not swim. Caught in the currents, they simply tumble along. This is an excellent way to fish the imitations. Any of the dead-drift tactics outlined in this book will work, but I prefer the long tippet technique (see chapter 10) and a strike indicator (see chapter 11) for all but the deepest water. This is the most sensitive tactic for use with smaller flies, and it allows the imitation to get down and stay down in the fast water areas where it should be fished. When bottom bouncing in deep fast water or when working an imitation deep in a pool, I use a sinking line. Great care must be exerted not to overtax the leader when striking a fish on a sinking line and light tippet. *Pull smoothly;* don't hit the fish with everything you've got.

One bright sunny afternoon just after lunch, I waded into the smooth flow of a knee-deep run to watch the movements of the *Brachycentrus* caddises that covered the bottom in row upon row. As I knelt there, a larva suddenly popped off the bottom and began floating downstream. Suddenly it halted in the currents a foot off the bottom. Perplexed at such behavior, I looked carefully; the larva had let itself out on a silk thread! As it hung there, occasionally twisting in the current, more larvae began to do the same. Whether they were feeding or whether it

Figure 8-5. Caddis larva letting itself out on silk thread.

was a type of dispersal, I don't know, but since then I've seen other caddises do the same. Midge and black fly larvae also let themselves out on silk threads. I've taken trout by simply letting a fly hang downcurrent on a long tippet just as those caddis larvae were doing.

When the caddis larva reaches maturity, it enters the pupal stage. The case-building species cement their cases to the bottom and seal off the front to form a pupation chamber; the Hydropsychidae pupate in their houses; the Green Rock Worm builds a pebble chamber on the bottom. Inside the pupal chamber, the insect undergoes a wondrous change. Wings develop, crumpled inside the pupal wing pads; the abdomen telescopes to form the smaller adult body; antennae lengthen twenty- to thirty-fold; mouthparts change from chewing to sucking; legs triple in length. In the end the pupal husk contains a fully developed adult.

Cutting out of the chamber with special mouthparts, the eager adult in pupal dress usually releases gases between the adult and pupal husks and explodes to the surface like a balloon. In *Challenges of the Trout,* Gary La Fontaine reports that the pupa drifts for some distance near the bottom before it finally generates the gases necessary for buoyance. Trout willingly pick off these drifting pupae. Once it has reached the surface, the pupal husk ruptures and the adult pops out, often ready for instant flight. This is the most vulnerable time in the

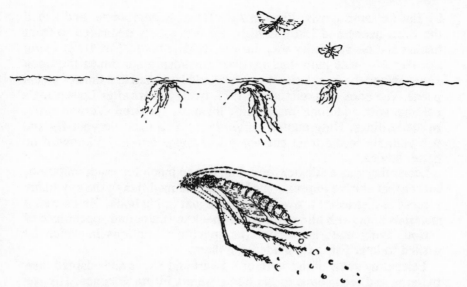

Figure 8-6. Many caddis pupae pop to the surface and the adults emerge rather quickly.

caddis's life; the trout devour them in great quantities, rolling and splashing in pursuit of these insects. Confronted with this caddis mania on the part of the normally shy trout, the angler often fails to recognize the feeding pattern and pounds the fish with dry flies, only to become more and more frustrated and puzzled by the constant refusals. It is a time for observation rather than a game of musical flies. Watch for the telltale signs of surface activity and use a screen to identify the hatch.

The timing of the hatch period is often not as concentrated as for the mayflies. Some species of caddises, like the American Grannom (*Brachycentrus* spp.), do hatch over a defined period of several weeks, but many other species, such as the Hydropsychidae caddises, hatch sporadically over the entire season. Others, like the Black Dancer (*Mystacides sepulcharlis*), have several overlapping generations per season, emerging in spring, summer, and fall. To make it even more complex, many species hatch at night. If you ever encounter a hatch of caddises after dark, you'll have some of the best night fishing you could ever experience. Because the caddises are hatching to some degree or other all season long, the trout are always exposed to this fare and readily accept a well-presented caddis pupa.

The best tactic I know for imitating the drifting pupa that suddenly leaps for the surface is the *Leisenring lift*. This method was developed by Jim Leisenring, who lived in Allentown, Pennsylvania, and fished the Broadheads and Little Lehigh. He was totally dedicated to trout fishing and his speciality was the wet fly. His book, *The Art of Tying the Wet Fly*, was published in 1941. In those tragic times the book never gained the popularity it surely would have had in a time of global peace. The book was reissued in 1971, twenty years after Leisenring's passing, with additional material by his most apt pupil, Vernon Hidy. In his writings, Hidy quotes Leisenring, "You must tie your fly and fish your fly so the trout can *enjoy* and *appreciate* it." I know of no better advice.

Leisenring was a stickler for detail, not so much for exact imitation, but for that elusive impression of life. He claimed this as the key to his success and stressed it over and over again in his book. He carried a materials book with him so he could check the color and appearance of various tying materials under the specific conditions in which he wished to later fish a fly made from them.

Leisenring knew of the work of Stewart and Skues and adapted their patterns and techniques to his home waters in the Poconos. His wet flies were his own creations, based on the sound entomological observations he made. These patterns were often wingless because, as he said, "I could always, and still can, catch more fish on a wingless imitation."

The basic wet fly method he used was to cast the fly upstream and slightly across on a short line and then keep just enough tension on it so there was no slack. When the line was downstream, Leisenring would check the rod and simply allow the fly to rise to the surface. He did not jiggle or otherwise manipulate the rod in any way. What he did do was to place his cast so that it arrived in a prime lie just as the current began lifting the fly from the bottom. The trout would see the fly bouncing toward him along the bottom and then suddenly begin rising to the surface right in front of his nose. The heavy creels Leisenring took are evidence of this method's effectiveness.

In his chapter on "Fishing the Flymph" ("Flymph" was the word he coined for emerger) Hidy suggests raising the rod high to bring the fly to the surface as it nears the feeding lie of a trout. This maneuver allows you to fish the fly across stream as well as down. It's a neat little trick to remember. Hidy also reemphasizes Leisenring's admonition not to allow slack in the line.

During a caddis hatch, use a floating line and a long tippet that allows the weighted pupal imitation to bounce along the bottom. The cast is reached up and across but not more than fifteen feet out unless you just can't get closer. The rod tip is raised high to take up the slack as the fly comes down; the fly should not be pulled up off the bottom by this lift. The lift also gets a good deal of the line up off the water and helps prevent drag. Mend only if absolutely necessary. As the fly passes in front, the rod is lowered to allow the line to move downstream at the same rate as the current. Keeping this slight tension on the line lets you feel even the lightest pickup. Watching the line point also helps detect strikes. When the rod has been lowered nearly to the water, the line will be hanging down and across and the fly will be at the critical point. The rod is lifted smoothly in a deliberate but unhurried fashion to pop the fly off the bottom and sweep it to the surface. Once at the surface the fly is allowed to swing across and hang downstream for a few seconds, then worked back up a few feet with the strip/tease just in case there's an indecisive trout watching it. When the fly comes up off the bottom, the trout usually grabs it hard. The high rod tip will help absorb the shock, but you've got to be ready too. Don't strike the fish; the rising rod will do all that's necessary.

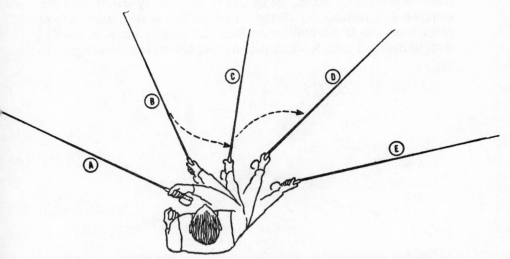

Figure 8-7. Leisenring lift during caddis hatch: (*A*) reach the cast up and across; (*B*) lift rod as line comes down; (*C*) follow line and lower rod; (*D*) lift rod in one smooth motion; (*E*) work fly back a few feet with strip/tease before making next cast.

The pupa can also be fished with a series of Leisenring lifts during a single drift. Cast up and across and let the fly drift for several feet so it can sink a foot or two; then lift it by raising the rod. Strip in the slack while dropping the rod tip. Let the fly drift on again for several feet; then lift again. Repeat until the cast is fished out. This is a good tactic for any stream area during a hatch or for just fishing the water. Repeated lifts can also be used in lakes; the angler just pauses between lifts to allow the fly time to sink. Use a long tippet and grease the leader butt to help you see the take. Be especially careful in quiet water areas not to disturb the water more than necessary when you make the lift.

If you see a fish feeding near the surface, place the fly upstream well above him and let it drift down; then jump it up right where you saw him rise. Another method that's sure-fire in riffles is to let the pupal imitation swing back and forth across the current. A riffle-hitched fly is potent medicine when the caddises are emerging in broken water.

Not all pupae emerge in the film; many swim to shore and crawl out of the water before the adult emerges. When these insects are emerging (mostly at night and at dawn), trout follow them into the shallows. You must be especially careful when fishing during these times so as not to spook the fish. The greased line method and the strip/tease are very good during such times.

Microcaddises (the Hydroptilidae and a few minute members of other families) occur across the United States in many waters. The one common denominator for all the microcaddises is their size. Adults range from two to six millimeters long, are usually black or mottled dark brown, and quite hairy. A rise to these insects is often assigned to

Figure 8-8. An adult microcaddis.

midge activity. Don't be fooled; use a surface screen to confirm the insect group. Additionally, fish will roll for the pupae and sip adults, sometimes with ambivalence, sometimes with exclusive and maddening preference for one or the other, thus requiring acute and constant vigilance from the angler.

Imitations representative of the microcaddises must be realistic in color, form, size, and in their suggestion of life. For the larva, a tiny Midge Nymph (see Midge Pupa in Appendix A) is most adequate, but these imitations are so small that presenting them in a bottom-bouncing drift is nearly impossible; so I rarely try to imitate the larva. The flowing legs, robust thorax, and shiny body of the pupa is superbly aped by a spider-type wet fly—the abdomen of floss, the robust thorax of dubbed fur, and the legs of grouse or similar soft hackle. These imitations are tied on sizes 18 to 24 hooks with an abdomen of dark brown, tan, green, dirty yellow, or orange; a dark brown thorax; and a brown or gray bird hackle wound one turn to form the legs. These patterns can be cast upstream and fished dead drift or twitched slightly on a greased leader. The slow draw can be deadly; the Leisenring lift is, without question, a most effective method, also.

Female caddises may deposit their eggs at the surface, but most species crawl beneath the water to oviposit. As the female submerges, an air bubble forms around her abdomen, trapped there by wing and body hairs, and transforms the dull Cinderella into a silver-gowned princess. Gravid females may also dive bomb into the water and swim rapidly to the bottom to deposit their ova. This unique habit was first described by Sid Gordon in *How to Fish from Top to Bottom*. While not strictly nymph fishing, imitating these ovipositing females is best done with a sunken fly rather than a dry fly. The best fly I've found is the Poly-Caddis; I fish it in one of three ways. First is the old standby—the down-and-across swing, letting the pressure of the current pull the fly under. This method is best in a choppy current where the broken surface lets the dragging fly dip beneath the film. The poly yarn wing traps a bubble of air as the fly dives. A riffle hitch on the fly allows it to run sideways to the current flow and thus present a side view to the fish. It's a trick worth trying.

In smoother, but still briskly moving water, I sometimes pop the fly by pulling it under and then letting it come to the surface. After it sits there for a few seconds, I pop it again. Trout will often jump out of the water and take the fly on the way down. When a good fish executes such a flamboyant maneuver, you've got to have nerves of steel to keep from pulling the fly away before he takes it. I'm usually so startled I forget to react at all.

Quiet pools are the hardest to work. Use a floating line and put a microshot a foot ahead of the fly. The tiny shot will pull the fly under. Don't jiggle the rod tip to impart action; work the fly with the rod tip high, stripping the line then pausing, stripping then pausing, etc. The shot will cause the fly to angle down when you pause, the strip will pull it back up again. It's a tactic that has taken fine trout.

Caddises *are* unique. Fishing them with consistent success requires an understanding of that uniqueness. With that understanding, when you encounter a good caddis hatch and the fish are splashing all around, you can be an active participant in the caddis mania.

Figure 8-9. Caddis mania.

Chapter 9

WINGSHOOTING AND THE JUMPING NYMPH

The Cretaceous was the last period of the Mesozoic era; it was the time of *Tyrannosaurus rex* and *Triceratops*, of marsupial mammals and the massive chalk deposits of England and Crete. The tremendous layers of chalk—which were built from the delicate, minute shells of marine foraminiferans—are the most significant geologic features of the period. The uncountable millions of microscopic shells are but loosely associated in the soft chalk. Over the millennia, the rains of England have cut into this material, forming a vast anastomosing network of underground waterways which emerge in places to form the fabled chalk streams. These immensely rich streams are the cradle of modern fly fishing and have continued since the days of Dame Juliana Berners to inspire fresh thoughts on angling.

Frank Sawyer was born into this magic land in 1906. His ambition was to become a river keeper—a warden, naturalist, and stream manager that maintains the highest quality angling possible. In 1925 he became an under-keeper, and in 1928 became the keeper for the Officer's Fishing Association. He still maintains its six-mile stretch on the Avon. Sawyer proved to be an innovative and careful worker. He collected insects on other rivers to strengthen the blood lines of those on the Avon. Hours spent watching the trout, the insects, and vegetation of the river showed him still further ways of improving the fishing. Out of these observations gradually came a theory on nymph fishing that he first applied to the bothersome grayling which inhabited the river, and then later, to the trout.

Through Sir Grimwood Mears, Edward Skues became aware of young Sawyer and his nymphing methods. The two men first met in 1945, when Skues was nearly ninety, and though Sawyer's ideas were radically different from his own in many ways, Skues saw the value of Sawyer's work and sponsored its publication. From those beginnings has come *Keeper of the Stream* and *Nymphs and the Trout*, both books

107

reflecting the rich store of angling knowledge harvested by Sawyer during his life-long tenure as river keeper and fly fisher.

To fit his angling method, Sawyer developed a series of alarmingly simple, yet deadly, flies. His fly tying methods reflect the hours of streamside observations: "Though a good copy of an insect is essential, this is not always enough; one should know what the fish ex-

Figure 9-1. Sawyer's p.t.

pect. . . ." Most of the patterns were developed to imitate swimming nymphs or nymphs that were actively moving about prior to a hatch. The flies are definitely impressionistic, stressing the general shape, color, and size of the naturals. Since the swimming insect keeps its legs tucked close to its body, Sawyer omitted legs but accentuated the thorax. Gills are represented by the materials of the body rather than being added separately, and the flies are weighted with copper wire to penetrate the film and sink quickly to the trout's level.

While Skues plied the film with delicate, hackled nymphs, Sawyer fishes the midwaters and the bottom with his streamlined, weighted representations. To compare the tactics is to compare apples and oranges. Both methods are good, both have accounted for many fine fish, and both are best applied when the fish can be seen. Sawyer's method, however, requires an ability to lead the trout with the fly at a sufficient distance so the imitation can sink to the fish's level. It's like *wingshooting*. In fast-moving water this requires masterful line handling to prevent drag.

Trout feeding on the bottom in shallow water often tip up at an angle, pushing their noses into the rubble as their tails break the surface. The approach to such tailing fish must be careful, but if you get into range and present the fly without spooking them, you're sure of a take. Pitch the fly in so it will sink to the trout's level a foot or two in front of him. Watch the fly if you can; if it's not visible, estimate its position by the speed of the current. When the fish opens and closes its mouth, gently lift the rod tip to pull the hook home. Skues put it so charmingly:

> . . . Delightful to ply
> The subaqueous fly,
> And watch for the wink underwater.

Figure 9-2. Tailing trout.

The leader must be long enough and fine enough so as not to frighten the fish. Generally I go to 150-inch leaders. Surprisingly enough, the little "plip" that the small, weighted nymph makes as it enters the water often gets the trout's attention and results in a take rather than a spooked fish. The line must be handled carefully to constantly minimize excess slack. Each cast *must* be the best you can make. Don't waste precious time fishing the water; this type of fishing is like quail shooting. When the birds bust out of cover, the first impulse is to fire into the center of the covey, but it doesn't work. You can't shoot at the flock; you have to pick out a bird and concentrate on it alone.

Spring creeks have some unique features that make them and their trout a challenge. First, the water is unusually clear and smooth-flowing. This means the trout are highly visible to predators, hence are more watchful and quicker to flee at the approach of danger. Charles Cotton's advice to "fish fine and far off" reaches across the centuries to the spring creek angler. Far off is not really a football field away as much as it is staying out of sight. By careful movements, concealment, and a lot of crawling, the angler can get quite close to trout in these

Figure 9-3. With care, the angler can get quite close to trout in spring creeks.

waters. Second, invertebrate life in the richly alkaline streams is usually smaller and far more abundant than in other waters. In addition to fishing small flies on the finest of leaders, the successful angler must be persistent. With the large number of food organisms drifting in his feeding lane, the trout need not move much to get all the fodder he wants, and your fly is only one of many. The constant, abundant drift of food, however, means the trout will be feeding almost continuously, and you'll get many opportunities at the fish. If the cast doesn't put the trout down, keep at him.

There are often sloughs or spring holes adjoining spring creeks. Here, since the water is not moving, the trout move—cruising in search of food. Again, get as close as possible; then watch the fish for a few moments to establish their cruising patterns. Use Sawyer's tactic, dropping the fly far enough ahead of your quarry so that fly and fish arrive in the same area at the same time. Time your cast so that its splash has subsided before the trout gets to the interception point. Watch for the wink underwater; it's your clue to tighten.

Such areas contain dragonfly and damselfly nymphs, waterboatmen, caddis larvae, and mayfly nymphs. But of special importance are the Chironomidae midges. They infest the vegetation and soft silt bottoms found in these sloughs. My favorite pattern for such places is the South Platte Brassy; this bare bones fly is the best pattern I've ever used to mimic the midge larvae.

Figure 9-4. South Platte Brassy.

Often the trout in the spring holes and sloughs are most sophisti-
cated, having learned about leaders and flies in the school of hard
knocks. They will frequently refuse the fly as it sinks, sometimes even
spooking when they sight it. For these fish, the *jumping nymph* is the
answer. Let the fly settle to the bottom and lie there, well in advance of
the fish. Keep the rod tip low, a couple of feet above the surface, and
pointed directly down the line. Strip out all slack. When the fish is a
foot or two from the fly, raise the rod tip slowly to jump the fly up off
the bottom. The fish rarely refuses.

Lakes were made to order for wingshooting and the jumping nymph.
Trout cruise in lakes and they can be plenty choosy. Many anglers drop
their caution when they see the vast expanse of the lake. Don't. Trout
in lakes are just as wild as trout in streams. Watch for the fish to be
cruising in or near weedbeds, along rocky points, near dropoffs, and so
on.

Adams Lake on the Vermejo Park Ranch in the Sangre de Cristo
Mountains of New Mexico is a classic trout lake. Where the road

Figure 9-5. East shore of Adams Lake with sloping sandy beach and weedbeds.

enters on the east, the shore slopes gently and there is a smooth sandy
beach. Wave action keeps the weedbed cleared from the first 15 to 20
feet of shoreward water, but beyond that, the plants extend out for 100
feet. At the north end of the lake, the shoreline rises abruptly, and
elodea grows to within a couple of feet of shore in this deeper water. A

Figure 9-6. Steep north shore of Adams Lake with deep water close to bank.

small feeder from Leandro Creek enters on the west shore, dropping swiftly down the abrupt slope and forming a silty delta. The south end of the lake is set in a cove that tapers gradually up into a grassy park where elk and mule deer feed in the evenings. Huge mats of filamentous green algae choke the shoreline in this area that is protected from the winds. The precipitous southeast bank begins in a rocky point at the mouth of the cove, and there are occasional snags sticking above the water near shore. Fish cruise the weeds, the rocky point, the currents of the delta, the open water of the cove, and around the snags.

The wingshooting and jumping nymph tactics work everywhere. Along the sandy east shore the angler stands back twenty feet from the

Figure 9-7. Sheltered cove on south shore of Adams Lake.

Figure 9-8. Snags along rocky point on southeast shore of Adams Lake.

water's edge and watches through polarized glasses. The leader is long and dressed so all but a couple of feet floats. The nymph is any of several—a Muskrat, a Red Brown, a small Wooly Worm, a p.t., a midge pupa, a Brassy—something that will match the damselfly or dragonfly nymphs, scuds, waterboatmen, caddis pupae, midge larvae, or small *Callibaetis* mayfly nymphs so prevalent in lakes. It is lying quietly on the bottom about two feet inshore of the weeds. The rod is low and the line lies straight across the grass and out onto the water. As the angler watches, he catches a glimpse of a fin, a shadow of a movement that glides toward his fly. The rod tip lifts gently, the fish takes.

Along the high banks on the north and southeast sides, fish are spotted in the three-foot-wide slot of open water next to shore. The angler is low and partially hidden behind a deadfall. The nymph pitches in well ahead of a fish which is moving toward the caster's position; the fish sees the fly and darts forward to seize it. Fish are also taken as they cruise over the weeds near shore. Later, glare prevents fishing to the trout out over the weedbed; so the angler's partner goes high up on the bank and hides behind a tree. From there the fish are visible and he calls out directions to the caster below.

A boat is used to position the anglers in the cove on the south end of the lake. The trout are sucking in the midge pupae that hang just under the film. The rises of each fish are like a string of pearls, giving away both the fish's direction of movement and the distance between takes. The cast leads the trout, and the fly lands where the next rise should

Figure 9-9. A boat is often necessary to get the best casting position in lakes.

be; the angler simply waits without moving the fly. The greased leader serves as a strike indicator.

Where weedbeds come all the way to the surface, there are often scattered pockets of open water. Trout will lie in these clearings and watch for insects in the surrounding weeds. Nancy, Jason, and I had camped near a reservoir situated high in a valley of the Little Belt Mountains of central Montana. As I walked down to the water, a flock of mallards rose noisily and flew off to the west. By this date in late July the water level had been drawn down about ten feet, and the feeder creek gurgled where it dropped down over the exposed bottom to form a narrow channel through thick beds of flowering water crowfoot. Ponderosa pine snags and piles of brush dotted the upper end of the reservoir.

The sun was just rising above the mountain peaks as the first trout of the morning took the p.t.; it was a solid twelve-inch fish. I worked along the shore, carefully fishing holes in the aquatic vegetation. The sequence was always the same. First the telltale bulge of a nymphing trout, then the cast. After the small weighted nymph had settled for several seconds, a gentle lift of the rod would bring a confident strike from the fish.

I crossed the creek and fished down the south shore of the reservoir. The sun was up now and the sky clear; killdeers ran across the mud, calling loudly. Trout were visibile, holding in the slow current of the

Figure 9-10. Pockets in weeds are often prime lies for trout.

channel, and the nymph was readily accepted when cast upcurrent and drifted deep along the edges of the aquatic vegetation. It was Sawyer's method, and it took brook trout to twelve inches and rainbows to fourteen inches.

Figure 9-11. Killdeers ran across the mud, calling loudly.

As the sun rose higher, the trout moved into deeper water and the fishing slowed. "Over sixty trout hooked, twenty-seven landed, in three hours," I thought, looking back at the reservoir as we broke camp. "It was an exceptional morning for wingshooting and the jumping nymph."

Chapter 10

THE LONG TIPPET

Scuds, sometimes called freshwater shrimp or sideswimmers, belong to the class Crustacea. Nearly all Crustaceans are aquatic: they breathe through gills; all have two pairs of antennae; and most of the body segments bear paired, jointed appendages. There are eleven orders of crustanceans in the fresh waters of the United States. Scuds belong to their own order, Amphipoda.

The majority of scuds are five to twenty millimeters in length. Their body is flattened at the sides and hinged like an armadillo. The head and first thoracic segment are fused to form a cephalothorax; the remaining seven segments of the thorax are free. There are six abdominal segments and a terminal segment, the telson.

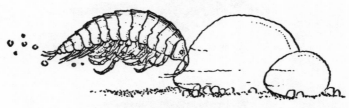

Figure 10-1. A typical scud.

Paired legs occur on each of the seven thoracic segments. The first two pairs of legs are club-shaped and used for grasping food. The other five pairs are simple walking legs. The organism holds the grasping legs and two pairs of walking legs pointed forward. The other three pairs of walking legs are held pointing rearward. Appendages on the abdomen are paired. The first three are bushy. All are held pointing rearward.

Like other crustaceans, the scuds are most active at night, during the dawn and dusk periods, and on overcast days. Using their walking legs, they crawl about the bottom trash or in beds of aquatic plants searching for food. During the bright hours of the day, scuds stay in vegetation or remain hidden in bottom debris. They are omnivores, consuming any type of dead plant or animal matter. Once in a while, however, they attack small, living water animals. When the scud swims, its body is held quite *straight*. The bushy abdominal appendages beat powerfully to propel the organism in an undulatory motion. Amphipods often roll onto their sides as they swim along; hence the name sideswimmer.

Breeding occurs throughout the warm seasons. Some females produce only one brood during their one-year life span, but some are as prolific as the proverbial rabbit. Eggs are kept in a special abdominal chamber of the female while they incubate. This helps protect the eggs from predation. It is an effective measure; amphipods can be amazingly abundant, reaching numbers in excess of 10,000 per square yard in the cress and elodea beds of spring creeks.

But they're not restricted to spring creeks. They occur in temporary ponds, permanent ponds and lakes, and all sizes of streams. Some inhabit lakes and streams in caves. Some are found in water having low carbonate content, but there are others that live happily in water of medium and high carbonate content. Interestingly enough, nearly all species are found in water less than three feet deep. *Hyallela azteca*, however, is often found at significantly greater depths, and *Pontoporeia affinis* has been found as deep as 1,000 feet in Lake Superior. Like trout, scuds require an abundance of dissolved oxygen, and with few exceptions, where you find trout, you will find the ubiquitous scud.

Gammarus limnaeus, *Hyallela azteca*, and *Crangonyx gracilis* are the three species usually found in trout waters. Their coloration varies like the rainbow. They may be pinkish tan, greenish, bluish gray, purple, dark brown, or reddish. Usually, though, the color will be pinkish tan, gray, or olive.

For the alert angler, scuds can provide some fascinating hours astream. The White River in Missouri and Arkansas is alive with scuds. Rainbow trout planted in the tailwater areas below dams grow heavy on this abundant fare. Most fish taken on flies fall to imitations fished to represent the scud. Many local anglers probe the gravel bars in the river where the bottom drops off sharply. They use a heavily weighted scud and strip/tease it along the bottom and up over the dropoff. Diametrically opposed to this weighty solution is the *long tippet* tactic. In this method, the fly contains just enough weight so it can sink quickly and is drifted along the bottom on a log tippet.

Long tippets are not new to fly fishing. Charles Cotton, who at Walton's invitation added a chapter on fly fishing to the 1676 edition of *The Compleat Angler*, admonished the fly fisher to "fish fine and far off." Skues warned of sacrificing delicacy to accuracy, but said the best anglers develop both. Although Sawyer only uses a two-foot tippet, he recommends a very light one so the fly may sink rapidly. Hewitt paid great attention to the tippet, recommending four to six feet of .005 to .003 gut for small nymphs; this was really fine for gut. In *Fishing the Nymph*, Jim Quick relates an interesting tip given to him by a friend: the use of a four-foot-long strand of fine, white silk thread as a tippet for bottom-bouncing small nymphs. The thread certainly gives the nymph freedom to move naturally, and this tactic was very successful for me on the Fisherman's Paradise water in Pennsylvania during the mid 1960s. Because the thread is so fragile and tends to come apart, you've got to change the tippet frequently. With the development of true diameter .004 and .003 limp monofilament, I stopped using the thread.

Though the past reflects a knowledge and use of long tippets, it has been Dave Whitlock who has perfected and popularized the long tippet tactic. Dave uses a five-weight, shooting head line, a long knotless leader spliced to the line with an epoxy joint, a long fine tippet, and if necessary, a strike indicator. The long leader and tippet allow the fly to sink rapidly and move naturally in the bottom currents. The line/leader junction or strike indicator serves to signal the take.

This is the best tactic I know of for bottom-bouncing with small nymphs. A long tippet can be used with Sawyer's method or when just fishing the water. For smooth flow, where the fish could be easily spooked, I use a long leader butt, such as that for the 100-inch leader designated in Table 1-2. For riffles, I cut the butt and tapered section back so they are only three feet long. You can make such a leader from the midsection of a commercial, tapered leader. Cut away the tippet; then remove the next three feet. Use this three-foot piece and add your own tippet. (Fig. 10-2). The tippet should be one and one-half to two times as long as the water is deep.

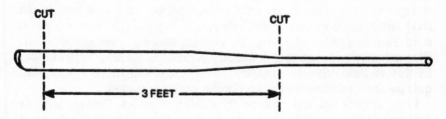

Figure 10-2. Cutting a commercial leader to make a three-foot butt for a long tippet leader.

A floating line is used with this technique, and a strike indicator (see chapter 11) may be affixed on the leader. Grease the fly line and any leader out to the indicator. The floating line, greased leader butt, and strike indicator will sit high on the surface where they can be easily seen. When a fish picks up the fly, there will be almost no drag from the long, thin tippet. This means the fish will hold the fly longer and increase your chances of a hookup. When the indicator pauses or jerks under, simply tighten the line. Often you'll get a common rock fish or moss fish, sometimes a stick fish; not infrequently, you'll get a trout. You can adjust the tippet length so that the fly is held just off the bottom by the floating line. This will decrease the number of snags you get.

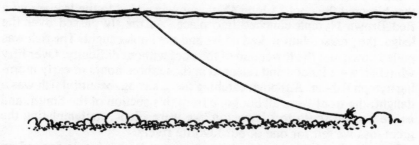

Figure 10-3. The long tippet allows the small fly to get down fast and stay down.

Stream-wise anglers know that the twilight hours of dusk and dawn are always good times for fishing. Biologically, this is related to a phenomenon known as *drift*. For some reason, possibly related to dispersal, there are definite periods when aquatic organisms leave the safety of the bottom and drift free in the currents. Although some drift occurs at all times, the peaks are at dawn and dusk. Hewitt and La Fontaine note this occurrence in their books and point out its significance to the angler. Such periods are well fished with the long tippet tactic.

The Smith River carves its way north through the Little Belt Mountains, eventually joining the Missouri. During hot August days it can be deceptively void of activity while the fish hold in pools under rock ledges in the canyon. But in early morning and again in the evening, the fish move to their feeding stations and provide superb fly fishing.

In the past, the Smith had surrendered numerous rainbows and browns to three pounds, especially during the morning, and I shivered from anticipation as I climbed down into the early morning shadows of the canyon and began to work the familiar currents of the pool. Dark water slid along the opposite canyon wall, pulling the streamer deep into the shadows of the overhanging rock. At the beginning of the erratic, pumping retrieve, a fourteen-inch rainbow took the fly. The fish fought well, jumping and streaking to the tail of the pool, yielding to the pressure of the rod with wild-eyed reluctance. Several minutes later I released him, thinking I'd found the secret, but the next half hour of fruitless casting convinced me that, indeed, I had not.

Well-worn trails, litter, and trout viscera along the streambank held the secret; this section of the river had been heavily fished since my last visit. The trout were gone. Feeling strangely melancholy and alone, I waded to shore and walked down the pool.

Silvery flashes showed whitefish were working along a rocky ledge that bisected the pool. A long 4X tippet was added to the leader and a Red Brown Nymph clinched into place. As the fly passed over the ledge, the greased butt jerked under and the hook caught. The fish was pulled down into the lower end of the pool without difficulty. Over fifty whitefish were landed and released in those three hours of early morning nymph fishing. Although catching these strong, beautiful fish was a delight, the trout were all but gone from this section of the Smith, and as we headed south to Livingston, we were silent, contemplating the great loss we felt for one of our favorite rivers.

Trout in the spring creeks of south central Pennsylvania depend on scuds as a winter food source. Charlie Fox reports that the fish begin in early winter to root out scuds and cressbugs from the aquatic plants. The trout pokes his nose into the plants, wiggles violently, then backs downcurrent a short ways and intercepts any organisms loosened by his rooting. Most of these fish are in fairly shallow water, and the long tippet tactic works well. The strike indicator is omitted since the fish can be seen, and the line and leader butt are greased with a paste-type floatant. The fly is presented up and across if possible, the cast being made just as the fish stops rooting in the weeds but before he drifts

Figure 10-4. Trout rooting for scuds in the elodea of the Letort.

downstream. This allows the fly a chance to get down and drift among the dislodged naturals. If the trout is close, watch for the flash of his mouth; if that's not clearly visible, watch for the fish to turn its head or for the leader butt to hesitate or draw under. The first trout I ever took from the Letort had been rooting and fell to a scud on a long tippet.

I spent my first year of college at the Mont Alto campus near Chambersburg, Pennsylvania. Bill Pfeiffer was director of the campus then and well known as an accomplished fly tier. He generously gave of his time to hold a fly tying class for some of us during the winter evenings; it greatly polished my techniques. Dr. Pfeiffer was also an observant and skilled angler. He was among the first to imitate and successfully fish the hatches of the minute White-Winged Black mayfly (*Tricorythodes* spp.).

It was not without a touch of nostalgia that I returned years later to fish the Trico hatch on Bill Pfeiffer's favorite stream, Falling Spring Creek. Cars jammed every side road and parking space available and anglers milled along the stream—some fishing, many watching. Nancy and I worked a short stretch of water during the hatch and we took several nice browns and rainbows. With the hatch over, most anglers left, and by 10 A.M. we had the river to ourselves. I replaced the 8X tippet with a long 6X point and clinched a weighted scud onto it. The

Figure 10-5. Bill Pfeiffer's beloved Falling Spring Creek has excellent populations of scuds.

water dumped around a corner and down a chute into a pool. By casting the fly up into the chute, it was carried deep into the pool with the plunging water. Lifting the rod high kept most of the line off the current and allowed me to steer the fly along just at the current's edge. I had better fishing with the scud and long tippet than I had during the Trico hatch.

Casting a long tippet is not as difficult as it may first appear. When using a big fly on the long tippet, a wide loop is necessary. The flimsy tippet just cannot support the big fly and will sag under its weight. An open loop will allow the sag without causing the fly to hang up on the line or rod. Be sure to watch the fly, as it often travels slower than the line, and you'll have to slow the timing accordingly. If you double-haul and move the rod very fast during the acceleration period on both backcast and forward cast, you'll be amazed at the big stuff you can toss around. The tension cast is also useful for pitching big flies on long tippets. For small flies, keep the loop tight, but haul on the line to give it the extra zip needed to hold up the long tippet. Sawyer pitches his nymphs by overpowering the forward cast so the line loop continues on over after it's straightened. The rod is stopped high to allow the fly time to flop over and get down ahead of the line. He uses a light line so it will fall quietly from the high position in which he stops it. It's a good method and not hard to learn.

A long tippet is useful in combination with other tactics. When the water is extra clear and the flies are small, a long, fine tippet will bring the most strikes—in the film or along the bottom. I prefer to use the long points for small flies because it allows them to move freely. Sullivan Lake along Silver Creek in Idaho is a crystal-clear, silt-bottomed haven for big trout. There were five fish cruising just ahead of me; all were over three pounds. I stood in a clump of brush and watched. They were feeding as they swung around in a twenty-foot-wide circle, intercepting small fare near the bottom. The water was only two feet deep, and these fish were not slow-witted. Four feet of 6X pointed the midge leader and a size 16 Brassy was carefully secured to the end. The number 4 line presented the fly delicately about fifteen feet ahead of the best fish. When the fish was a foot away, I jumped the nymph off the bottom and saw the wink underwater. The trout ran across the pool and under a mass of fallen branches. When I put gentle pressure on him, he leaped up through the cover and broke the tippet. That fish had been around, but he still fell for the jumping nymph and the long tippet.

Chapter 11

STRIKE INDICATORS AND SHOTGUNNING FOR TROUT

I had come home a pilgrim, back to the state of my birth to fish its most hallowed waters. And now it was raining. Not the gentle spring rain that brings joy to the soul, but a heavy, determined pounding, each drop driving my spirits deeper within. The Yellow Breeches would be unfishable by morning; perhaps the Big Spring would suffer less. I pulled the down bag against my face and slept.

Morning saw no letup of the rain, and I finally arose at nine, determined at least to see these great streams. On the way to Newville, I crossed the Letort and was heartened by its clear, smooth currents. Just maybe, things were looking up. In town, the Big Spring was littered with old tires and other castoffs, but as the road wound upstream, I felt a peaceful excitement in the old willows and beds of watercress that graced the banks. Slow, deep flats spilled their contents into jingling riffles; the river slid beneath the pads of cress and murmured among the rocks.

As by design, the rain slackened and the dark clouds marched on to leave a peaceful drizzle from a brightened sky. I parked the truck and got out to see the river. Although it's water that sustains a stream, there is union between this fluid and the earth through which it flows. In concert they determine the spirit and character of a stream; its moods; its very soul. Here before me was a watershed of serene grace and proud heritage—pure, clean water easing its way through a land that comforted and shaded it with massive willows and luxuriant pads of watercress.

There are times in angling when everything just *feels* right. This was one of those times. The relief of seeing the stream in a fishable condition and the hope of a clearing sky were combined with the sweet nostalgia of childhood's home and the adventurous prospect of fishing a new stream. I was happy and excited.

Upstream, dancing riffles lapped along a stone riprap and disappeared beneath the cress to emerge smoothed and quiet-flowing. It would be a good place to start. A long strand of 5X was carefully

Figure 11-1. Riffles lapped along a stone riprap and disappeared beneath the cress.

knotted to the leader and a Red Brown Nymph clinched in place. The first cast was good, but glare prevented me from seeing the take until it was too late. The line was dipping under before I reacted, and the big brown greyhounded across the top and dislodged the poorly set hook. My heart pounded at his size. If there were more fish in there like that one, I'd have to overcome the problem of glare. Removing the fly, I slipped a small, fluorescent orange, cork strike indicator onto the leader and secured it half way up the butt. The line reached over the water to the head of the stonework, and the nymph sank quickly and was carried beneath the cress bed. The little cork was visible, floating along just at the edge of the plants. Suddenly it paused. This fish was a handsome 2¼-pound brown that surrendered as he had fought, throwing water into my face when I knelt to remove the barb from his mouth.

Again the cast, the drift, the pause, the fish. The trout slid downstream beneath the vegetation, and its large size was not apparent until gentle pressure eased it from cover. Large red spots highlighted its silvery brown flanks touched with black and azure points. On a short line the fight was strong, but one-sided; I quickly brought the four-pound hen to net, saving its strength for the release.

The next few casts gave no results as I manipulated the line to get it farther back under the cress. Finally the line was swept to the inner recesses of the bed, emerging directly across stream from me. As the indicator jerked forward, the rod lifted and the trout was hooked. Not as relaxed as the first big female, this one ran upstream, then crossed and jumped several times. A determined fish is never easy, but the rod met her fury with flexibility and strength. More delicately gowned than the first, this four-pound hen responded quietly as I removed the hook and steadied her in the currents; rested, she slipped away.

Downstream, the river beckoned, and I walked along quietly. "Yes, I see why you call, where the fly must fall, how the line should drift, the snag to be avoided." The nymph swept toward the cress and was met by the fish. It was a strong 2¾-pound brown that fought with more skill and bravado than the others; it was a fitting way to end the morning's angling.

Strike indicators are by no means new to angling or to fly fishers. Dame Juliana Berners described a series of various-sized cork floats for angling. Father Walton was not without his floats, either. Skues used the leader as a strike indicator, watching for it to "draw under." Hewitt recommended tying pieces of white floss on the leader to help see the take. Ray Bergman discussed the use of large, bushy dry flies as indicators while nymphing and also pointed out that a "bit of cork painted a color you can see will signal when a fish has taken" the nymph. Modern fly fishers have embraced the concept. Dave Whitlock uses a short piece of fluorescent fly line at the line/leader connection as a strike indicator, and the Cortland Line Company manufactures a floating line with built-in indicator.

Strike indicators are not necessary or even useful in all nymphing situations, but if the nymph is to be dead drifted in choppy currents, or if glare prevents seeing the leader, a marker is invaluable. I prefer cork indicators because even in the tiniest sizes they float very well. They can be rapidly affixed to the leader, positioned at the most advantageous point, and can be quickly removed. In addition, these small, delicate corks don't interfere with the line loop during casting.

To make a cork indicator, use a cylindrical popper cork ⅝ inch long by ¼ inch in diameter. First, cut it in two, crossways; then use a red-hot needle to burn a hole lengthwise through each half. The charred material in the hole is firmer than the cork and makes an excellent passageway for the leader. After you've burned holes in a dozen or so corks, round the ends slightly with a file (Fig. 11-2). For ease of handling during painting, string them on a piece of leader material. The corks are given a spray job with decoupage sealer to plug up the pores,

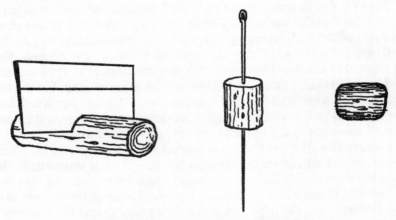

Figure 11-2. Making cork strike indicators.

and when dry, given two coats of spray enamel. Fluorescent orange and chartreuse are the most visible colors.

Slide the strike indicator onto the leader and jam a piece of toothpick into the hole to hold the cork in place. After the cast settles to the water, rivet your attention on that little marker and watch its *speed*. The weight of the fly may pull the indicator under a few inches, but its *speed* won't change. When a trout intercepts the fly, the indicator will slow, stop, or jump upstream.

The Peshtigo! I was new to Wisconsin, but all my angling life I had heard tales of this river; now I was going to fish it. Jim Dalnodar had invited me to share his favorite water, and I slept restlessly. We left at sunrise and headed east through Antigo. Our eagerness to be astream was reflected in our constant babbling. Trout streams we had fished, catches we had made, favorite flies, the grace of a prized rod, and the woes of poor-quality waders made the two-hour drive pass quickly. "This is it," Jim said, "the burnt bridge. We'll split up here." He drove me a mile upstream and let me out with careful instructions on

The leaves were just taking on the deep green of summer and wild flowers dotted the forest floor. Mosquitoes hummed annoyingly, but the air was sweet with the new season and the sky radiant with the morning light. The river gurgled and splashed its greeting before I saw it. There was a variety of deep-water holds broken by room-sized boulders and slashed with gravel bars. Two hours later, the big stonefly nymph had picked up only three small fish, and I headed back to our prearranged rendezvous. Jim was there, and he was too quiet.

"How was it?" he asked.

"I like the water," I allowed, "but I only took three small ones. How'd you do?"

"Twenty-nine," he replied, trying to be casual.

"Twenty-nine!" I choked. "Where were you fishing, in a hatchery?"

"Right above the bridge," he noted. "Tough wading in there though."

The water Jim had been fishing was a long choppy riffle with several runs in it. He'd been fishing with two nymphs and a short line. "Now I see why you did so well," I poked. "You shotgunned them." Jim laughed and we headed upstream for another riffle he knew about.

In riffles with any depth (a couple of feet or more) the trout tend to disperse and hold over the entire area. Any bottom depresssions or sizable obstructions will provide plenty of shelter, food organisms are everywhere, and the choppy surface gives the fish security from predators. Such areas are prime trout habitat and should be fished carefully and thoroughly.

The broad pattern of pellets from a scattergun is designed to saturate a given area at short range. The *shotgun* tactic is likewise designed to cover a specific area extensively within a short casting distance. This is the most efficient and most productive way to fish riffly areas.

Since the trout can be anywhere, the angler should approach the water in a systematic way rather than hopscotch about in a random fashion. If the water is a broad, uniformly deep stretch like that shown in Figure 11-3, the angler would enter at point *A* and deliver a series of twenty to thirty casts to area 1, then repeat the casting sequence to area 2. He then would move to point *B* and cast to areas 3 and 4, and so forth, covering the water in a gridlike pattern. Each area is about ten by ten feet and should be about ten feet upstream of the angler's position. The broken surface allows you to wade quite close to the fish. If the stream is very wide, the angler wades to the left or right to fully cover the water. The casts will come rather rapidly, since the fly only floats ten feet or so before it is picked up for the next cast. In this way, the angler works upstream, always fishing from water that has been fished. If distinct channels are present, the angler should stay just to one side of the deep water and thoroughly cover the channel (Fig. 11-4). This saturation approach assures that every nook and cranny of the bottom is exhaustively searched by the nymph.

A floating line is mandatory since it is visible and easily lifted from the surface. The casts are made upstream and the casting distance kept around the twenty-foot mark. Once it settles to the water, the line will immediately begin to float toward you. Keep the slack out of the line by

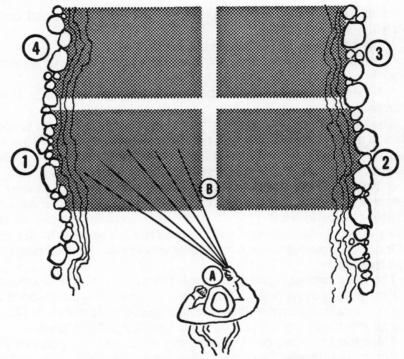

Figure 11-3. Shotgunning a broad riffle.

lifting the rod tip and drawing back on the line with the line hand. When the rod tip is vertical, flip the tip forward to make a roll cast pickup and deliver the next cast.

In smooth flows, this tactic can be used without a strike indicator, but in choppy water, that bright marker is almost a necessity. The distance from fly to indicator is a function of current speed and the depth you wish to fish. If the fish are nymphing just below the surface, set the strike indicator two or three feet from the fly. To drift the nymph along the bottom, set the indicator at a distance equal to two to three times the water's depth.

For bottom bouncing, the fly must sink quickly, and weighted nymphs are most desirable. Microshot or moldable lead affixed to the leader will help get the fly down fast and keep it down. The leader can be designed to assist in the rapid sinking of the fly. Use a fairly light tippet (4X or 5X for a size 10 nymph) and make it about one and one-half times as long as the water is deep. This long, light tippet will allow the fly to get down quickly and will not tend to buoy it to the

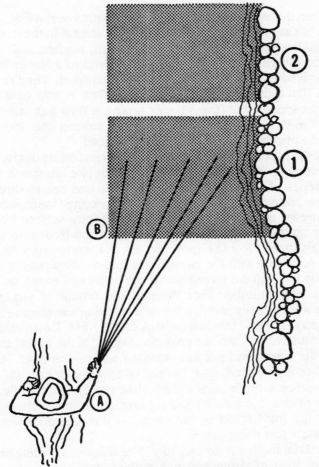

Figure 11-4. Shotgunning a channel.

surface. After putting the strike indicator on the leader, apply a paste-type floatant to that portion of the leader from the fly line to the indicator. This high-floating section of the leader will make strike detection and pickup easier.

The San Juan River of northwestern New Mexico, like the mythical Phoenix, dies in fire only to be reborn from the ashes. It spills from the heights of the San Juan Mountains into the torrid desert below, where it is greatly warmed and charged with silt. Barricaded by the Navajo Dam near Aztec, the river forms Navajo Lake, whose depths cool the water and settle out the silt. The cold, clear water is released from the base of the dam. Even during summer this water rarely runs over 44° F., giving rebirth to a twenty-mile stretch of superb trout stream in the heart of a sun-scorched landscape dominated by sagebrush, washes, and mesas.

"You'll be surprised at its richness," Bob Pelzl told Nancy and me when we arrived in Albuquerque, "and with its trout. They're deep-bodied fish that fight like tigers. The river's flow is now held at 600 cubic feet per second, but it was better when the flow was maintained at 1,200." The stories he told of past catches seemed like fairy tales, even with the photographic evidence he produced.

We spent the first few hours exploring the river, feeling out its mood and prospecting for its mother lode of trout. In late afternoon we arrived at a series of riffly runs where the water was one to three feet deep and the bottom was pockmarked with watering-trough-sized depressions strewn among stony shoals. The choppy surface currents that hid the bottom structures would also give the trout a feeling of security. This looked like the spot, and the few exploratory casts we made were rewarded with the strong pulls and heady jumps of silver-sided rainbows. Darkness forced us off the river, and as we stumbled clumsily on river-numbed feet through the tangle of streamside willows, we were already plotting the next morning's angling session.

The thin gray light of dawn saw us back on the river. Down vests and long johns insulated us from the cold morning air of the desert and the icy chill of the water, and our full attention was on the trout. A total lack of surface activity indicated the use of nymphs, but the dull light and riffly currents made strike detection nearly impossible. The hodgepodge of possible holding and feeding lies in this section of the river meant the trout could be anywhere. It was a perfect setup for strike indicators and shotgunning for trout.

We worked the mother lode carefully. The fish were feeding heavily in the umber light of dawn and our probing casts were constantly finding fish. Suddenly the sun came crowding over the mesa; the feeding slowed, then stopped. The day heated quickly, and we shed our outer garments as we headed back to the van.

Several anglers were just arriving for the day.

"Get any?" they queried.

"Yes, on nymphs," we said.

"How'd ya fish 'em?" they pressed.

We looked at each other and smiled. "Shotgunning," we replied. "Strike indicators and shotgunning."

Chapter 12

SECRET OF THE WOOLY WORM

Opening morning dawned too early, and Bob Pils, Russ Wiskowski, and I lay in our down bags watching the sun sparkle in the heavy frost and chattering about our prospects for the new season. Excitement that had been building over the long winter finally forced us from the van, and we drank in the sweet north woods air. Fishermen were on the stream now, and we could see their rods working as they drifted in and out of view among the white pines and alders. Breakfast over, we scoured the utensils and looked to the angling gear. Heavy wool socks were followed by long johns, field pants, wool shirts, and turtlenecks. Waders protested stiffly as they were unfolded and pulled on, and with clothes-stifled limbs, we shouldered into our jackets. During this time we were bantering about fly patterns, lines, and techniques, and as the rods were uncased, a consensus was reached: Each would use a different approach. One would fish the runs with a Blacknose Dace and sinking line, another chose to dredge the pools with weighted nymphs and hi-density line, and the other would work the pools with weighted wet flies and a floating line. The Dace moved the first trout, but the big weighted nymphs made the first solid connection. The stomach pump revealed that the fish had been feeding on dragonfly nymphs and fishfly larvae; he had taken a Hair Leg Wooly Worm. As the embers of the evening's fire glowed warmly on our tired faces, we recounted a most successful opening: four trout over two pounds, the largest a heavy-bodied four-pounder taken just at lunch time. All the big fish had fallen to the Wooly Worm.

There are several groups of aquatic insects that lend themselves to imitation by the Wooly Worm. The Metaloptera, encompassing fish flies, alderflies, and dobsonflies; Cole-optera, or beetles; and Lepidoptera, or moths, have Wooly Worm-shaped larvae. In addition to their normal complement of thoracic legs, these insects bear filamentous lateral appendages on their abdomens; a few beetles lack these appendages (see Appendix B).

In my samplings, I have never found any one group of the wooly worm larvae to be the dominant form in trout waters; collectively, though, these insects are frequently as abundant as one or another of the more popularized insects. In streams, the Megaloptera occur in rocky or gravelly runs and riffles where they crawl about in search of prey. The beetles and moths are creatures of calm pools, backwaters, beds of vegetation, and stream edges. In ponds, wooly worm larvae are generally found in bottom trash and pads of vegetation. Thus, one or another of these insects will be present, regardless of the feeding area of the trout.

In addition, many of these larvae live for several years before pupating. This means there is a year-round supply of them. Most are large (twenty to ninety millimeters). Their size and continual presence makes them a choice tidbit for even the largest trout. And trout seem well acquainted with this diverse, yet similar-appearing, fare. Examination of stomach contents has shown that trout take these wooly worm larvae throughout the year. This never concentrated, but continuous, fodder is the secret of the Wooly Worm; its effectiveness is not based on representing one life form but several similar-appearing ones that occur as a consistent item in the trout's diet.

Although the standard Wooly Worm is an excellent fly, I have come to prefer a more realistic impression. The pattern is tied with fuzzy yarns such as mohair and mohlon and with hair, rather than hackle, legs (see Hair Leg Wooly Worm in Appendix A). This imitation has proved to be very successful when fished dead drift along the bottom of rocky stretches or crawled slowly among the bottom trash of pools and ponds. Twitched gently among aquatic plants, it has taken some fine fish.

The main problem in fishing big nymphal imitations along the bottom of fast-water reaches is getting them to stay down. One solution is to wrap lead fuse wire along the hook shank before constructing the fly. Such a practice has been criticized because it supposedly makes the fly look lifeless in the water. This might or might not be the case; it depends upon the action of the natural, the materials used in the fly, its method of construction, and where and how it's fished. My angling experiences have consistently led me back to the theories of Grant, Rosborough, and Atherton. George Grant convincingly insists that hair legs are best for a fly that's fished in moving water since they don't collapse yet still move in the currents. "Polly" Rosborough is famous for his ideas on tying fuzzy-bodied nymphs, and John Atherton put forth the concept of impressionism in fly patterns. It is these concepts on which the Hair Leg Wooly Worm is built. Although it is weighted and simply dead drifted in fast water, the hair legs, fuzzy body, and impressionistic shape give it a most lifelike appearance. When twitched in slow water, the legs and fuzzy body pulse and tremble with a living quality.

Charlie Brooks is a retired Air Force major living just outside West Yellowstone, Montana. He lives there because the rivers of that region give him an opportunity to do what he loves most: fish for big trout with nymphs. I have read his books—*Larger Trout for the Western Fly Fisherman*, *The Trout and the Stream*, and *Nymph Fishing for Larger Trout*—through and through, listened to him lecture, and chatted with him. I've always come away with the feeling that this man knows of what he speaks. But like all anglers, "I'm from Missouri"; show me it works and I'll believe it. The big fish that Bob, Russ, and I took that opening morning fell to the Brooks method; I'm a believer.

This method is very similar in concept to the Leisenring lift, but the form is different. First, the Brooks method is for big flies fished on stout leaders. Second, it employs a high-density sinking line. Begin with a short cast, twenty feet or so, pitching it up and across so the fly will drift down about six feet in front of you. End with the tip of your rod low and aimed right out the line. As the line sinks and comes down, the point where the line enters the water will move downstream. Move the rod tip downstream *just ahead* of that point while slowly raising the rod. When the point is directly in front of you, the tip of the rod should be about four feet off the water.

This lift is the most difficult part of the tactic since it requires a bit of sensitivity to what the line is doing. You want to lift just enough to keep out the slack but not so much that you move the fly. With the Leisenring lift, the line is floating, and it's quite easy to tell what's happening. With the Brooks method, the line is sliding along the bottom and totally invisible except where it enters the water. The line is actually bowing upstream (Fig. 12-1). The slow bottom currents hold the line back while the faster surface currents push against the line where it enters the water. The slack produced as the line comes down feeds the forming bow. If you didn't lift out the slack and lead the line, the bow would get larger and larger. The large bow would allow the faster surface currents to push against more line and pull the fly downstream faster than the bottom currents were moving (Fig. 12-2).

When the line goes past you, continue to lead it and lower the rod tip at the same rate the current takes the line. The fly will tumble along naturally until you've lowered the rod on the downstream side; then

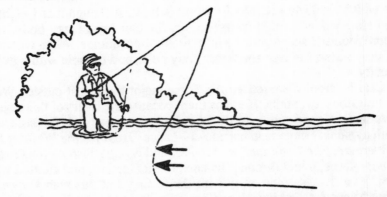

Figure 12-1. Lifting the line and following it keeps the upstream bow small.

Figure 12-2. Without the lift the line develops a large bow.

the pressure of the water on the bow will begin to accelerate the fly down and across. At first the fly will move along the bottom, but then, when the line is nearly straightened out in the currents, the fly will swing to the surface (Fig. 12-3).

Fish may take the fly at any point during the drift, but most take the fly at some point after the line begins to pass your position, especially as the fly is swinging down and across. You can't daydream when you're using this method; every fiber must be ready to strike if a fish socks the fly. And sock it they do. First of all, in the fast water, the fish has only a short period of time to nab the fly; so he rushes out and grabs it. Second, there's the pressure of the water on that sinking line. You'll feel the strike all right. When you do, pull the hook home with everything you've got. You have to overcome the resistance of the bow in the sinking line; this is no time for a gentle lift of the rod tip.

Figure 12-3. The Brooks method: (A) cast upstream; (B) lift rod and lead the line; (C) lower rod and lead the line as it passes you; (D) wait and allow the line to swing to your side before making the next cast.

After each drift, let the line completely straighten in the currents and swing across to your side; then slip out another foot or so of line and pitch the fly upstream with the tension cast. The farther upstream you cast, the higher you have to lift the rod as the line comes down. On the longest casts (thirty to forty feet), the rod will have to be held high overhead. After you've made twenty to thirty casts in one spot, lengthening each one a foot or so, move up or down a short ways and begin again.

Brooks uses this tactic for deep, fast runs, and at the head of a pool where the rapids dump in. Trout lying at the lip are watching for food items to come tumbling down out of the fast water. You can locate the lip by the shape and size of the waves. In the rapids, the waves are large and often curl upstream at their tops. As the water pours into the pool, it spreads out and its velocity decreases. There are still waves for some distance, but they are smaller and more choppy-looking. Stand about six feet upstream from the lip and probe the flies down over it. This is a very effective method.

The leader used with a sinking line in fast water should be short; I like leaders about four feet long with a two-foot tippet. The short leader is necessary to prevent upwelling turbulence from buoying the fly too far above the bottom. The tippet should be stout. For the big weighted Mono Stonefly Nymphs, Muskrats, Hair Leg Wooly Worms, and so on, don't fool around. Go directly to 0X or 1X. When you strike, the resistance of the sinking line is just too much for light tippets.

The heavy leader point used when fishing big nymphs may tend to boss the fly and not allow it total freedom of movement. This effect can be overcome by using a Duncan loop to secure the fly to the tippet. The knot is tied as shown in Figure 12-4, and the loop is not snugged up against the fly. The nymph rotates around on the loop; when a fish

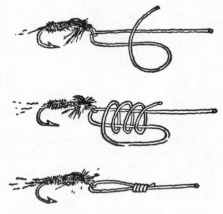

Figure 12-4. The Duncan loop.

takes the fly, the loop slides shut. It is easily reopened. Don't worry about the strength of this knot; it is one of the strongest I know.

For bottom bouncing, I often use two big nymphs. Frequently, they are different flies, but if I take several trout in a row on one of them, I replace the other with a fly like the one the fish have been taking. To rig for two flies, tie the tippet to the leader with a double blood knot and let the short end of the *heavier* material stick out of the side of the knot about six inches (Fig. 12-5). One fly is attached to this short end and one to the point of the tippet. Two nymphs can be tough to cast in a normal fashion, but if you use a tension cast or cast with a wide loop

Figure 12-5. The dropper arrangement for fishing two nymphs.

and double haul, you won't experience much difficulty. Do check the flies occasionally to be sure they haven't become tangled or the hooks dulled on the rocky bottom.

In heavy, deep flows, even high-density line and weighted flies often aren't enough to reach the bottom. Additional weight such as split shot, twist-on lead strips, fuse wire, or moldable lead putty may be necessary. I like shot and the moldable lead putty the best. Removable shot is great, but it can be cast right off the leader. The best way to use it is to tie the leader *around* the shot with a simple overhand knot. Pull the knot tight; then pinch the shot closed (Fig. 12-6). The leader isn't

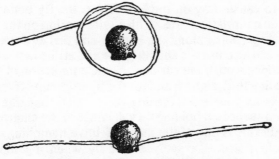

Figure 12-6. Using removable shot.

weakened because the knot isn't pulled completely shut; it's around the shot. The shot won't come off because the knot is holding it on.

For delicate weight, I use microshot, but I'm coming more and more to prefer the moldable lead putty. It can be shaped into any form and size. I usually mold it over a knot to keep it from sliding along the leader. There is still one time when microshot is best; that's for adding weight at the fly. One of those tiny shots can be pinched immediately above the clinch knot and it won't interfere with the fly or the casting loop. When shot is put any distance above the fly, its momentum causes it to go farther than the fly during the cast. This results in tangles. The tension cast or open loops help alleviate this problem.

Fishing these large imitations is not the delicate sport that fly fishing is often said to be; rather, it is more akin to weightlifting and wrestling mountain man-style. A number seven, or heavier, line and an eight-foot, or longer, rod handle this weighty problem best. After a day's bottom dredging with this outfit, it is only the satisfaction of large fish taken that coaxes the angler back to this tiring method.

To provide some relief, I use a lead-tip line, splicing five to six feet of thirty-six-pound test, plastic-coated, lead-core line to a fluorescent orange shooting line. The leader is attached directly to the free end of the lead-core line. Again, keep the leader short and stout; this is an outfit for big flies and big fish.

Cast quartering upstream as with the Brooks method, and either reach the cast or immediately mend the shooting line upstream. As the current carries the lead tip toward you, lift the rod to take up the slack in the shooting line. As the line passes your position, lower the rod at the same rate as the current is carrying the line. The reach or mend provides a slack line and allows the tip to sink without current drag pulling it upward off the bottom. Lift and lower the rod to keep just enough tension on the line so a strike can be detected but not so much tension as to cause drag on the line. Thus, the fly bounces along the bottom at the natural flow rate. With a little tension on the line, you can feel the lead tip rolling along the bottom and feel any strikes that may occur. You can also use the shooting line as a strike indicator, watching it where it dips through the surface. At the completion of the free drift, wait for the line to straighten and for the fly to get up off the bottom and swing across to your side. Placing the cast so that this rising swing occurs near a suspected holding lie will enhance the chances of a strike. Be prepared! This is one of the most effective nymphing techniques; a trout will often strike savagely at the fly when it jumps up off the bottom in front of its nose. When the fly is straight downstream, strip in the line, leaving about ten feet to pick up for the next cast.

You've got to be a little careful about casting this outfit. The lead-core line moves more slowly through the air than does a fly line. Watch the backcast to be sure the line is nearly straight before you begin the forward cast. Use an open loop and haul the line to keep it moving as fast as possible. The tension cast works very well with this line. Remember to strip in most of the line before you cast; that thin running line just can't carry enough energy to turn over the lead tip.

In very swift, broken flows, the trout must stay in the sheltering lee of boulders and other obstructions. The fly has to come down close to these sheltered pockets because the trout just won't go very far for food in the strong currents. The lead-tip line is very effective for "picking the pocket," getting the fly down quickly in the fast water and holding it down as it drifts along. Try to get the fly right at the edge of the pocket, not into it (Fig. 12-7). Present it from whatever angle you can; in the strong currents, you can't always get below the lie. The floating, fluorescent shooting line is easily mended or held high to prevent drag and serves as a strike indicator. It's tough fishing, but rewarding. Other anglers often pass up such places because they are so

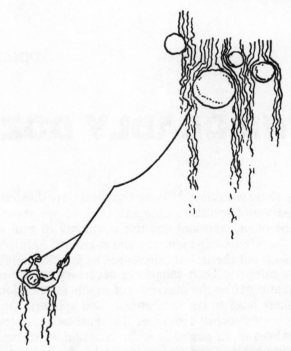

Figure 12-7. Fishing the edges in rapids with a lead-tip line.

hard to fish, and consequently, the fish run bigger than in more accessible spots.

Short lead points can be added between a normal fly line and the leader to help get the fly down in moderate currents. They are useful on sinking or floating lines. I have found them especially good where there are shelves dropping into deep water out of moderate, shallow currents. The lead point will roll along the bottom and then drop right off the shelf.

The Brooks method, heavily weighted flies, lead on the leader, and lead-tip lines are special tactics for deep, fast water. They are not the most delicate or poetic ways of fly fishing, but they do take big fish.

Appendix A

THE DEADLY DOZEN

Taxonomists, those who classify living organisms, are divided into two camps: lumpers and splitters. Lumpers tend to see gross characteristics as the most important and use taxonomy to gain a general oversight of the relationships among various groups. Splitters, on the other hand, seek out the tiniest differences as justification for establishing a new category. Both camps are necessary to achieve a balanced view that provides the maximum of usable information.

Nymph fishers have to be both lumpers and splitters. On the one hand, there are very special conditions that must be understood about specific organisms if the angler is to be consistently successful; the bottom-hatching habit of the *Epeorus* nymphs, for example. On the other hand, knowing that one fly is useful as a general imitation of several organisms will also increase angling success. But of course you have to know the details of the organisms before you can know if they're alike. Detail and overview fit like hand in glove.

If you go through the insect keys in Appendix B and read the descriptions of various organisms, you will note similarities, even though the insects may be in widely separated taxonomic groups. For instance, note the silhouette of burrowing mayflies, dobsonflies, fishflies, alderflies, aquatic moths, and aquatic beetles; true, there are structural differences, but the overall picture is one of similarity. Trout *are* selective to nymphs, and remember, selectivity is a function of size, color, motion, and silhouette. The vast majority of nymphs fall into twelve basic silhouette families. For each family, I have given the type pattern, variations that can be made on it, the most used sizes and colors, and the organisms imitated. With this selection of nymphs, you can be at home on any water.

Many of the flies I've included are strongly impressionistic. In this sense, I have been greatly influenced by the late John Atherton, American artist of note and author of the classic angling text, *The Fly and the Fish*. Atherton was fully aware of the impressionistic artists

140

who attempted to give the immediate and overall feeling of the subject *as it interacted with the surroundings*. He saw this as the goal that the fly tier was also trying to achieve.

When designing artificials, the tier should strive to develop the impression of life by selecting materials that most closely mimic the appearance of the particular structure being imitated. For nymphs, the body is the most prominent feature. Many materials are usable for bodies. Lacquered floss gives the appearance of depth and radiance, and flat monofilament is excellent in this regard; but furs and hairs are the best known and most widely used body materials. Fur dubbing is easily applied, has the translucency of life, and can be blended to yield any color. Blending is to be preferred since the various colors highlight one another, giving the fly the living glow so convincingly demonstrated by the Impressionists. When blending, I start with the base color I want, then add small amounts of component colors to achieve the desired shade and add highlights.

As Atherton mentions, impression is also attained through silhouette. Trout see silhouettes, but lack the visual acuity to see fine detail. When silhouette is coupled with materials that give the impression of life, the fly is sure to be successful. Polly Rosborough's engrossing little volume, *Tying and Fishing the Fuzzy Nymphs*, is a master study in combining these two necessary ingredients. I've read it many times and I'm still finding new insights into his concepts of the fuzzy nymphs.

I've mentioned some dyed items that may not be readily available, so I'm giving the dye formulas below. Simply mix up the solution as indicated, heat it to boiling, and immerse the material for the given time. Rinse well in cold water to wash out any extra dye. Prepare the dye bath with two quarts of water, one teaspoon of salt, and the recommended amount of Rit dye: t. = teaspoon, tbs. = tablespoon. For flat mono, dye 15-30 seconds *only*. For rabbit fur, pheasant tail, and goose quill, dye 2-4 minutes.

Tan: 2 t. tan
Gray: 1 t. gray
Olive: ½ t. olive green, 1 t. gold
Green: 1 t. jade green
Orange brown: 1 t. gold and ½ t. cocoa brown
Rusty brown: 2 t. cocoa brown
Black: 1 tbs. dark brown and 1 tbs. black

THE RED BROWN NYMPH

This fly evolved in 1972; I had been experimenting with hair legs and had found a way of applying them that was practical and fast. Doug

Swisher and Carl Richard's book, *Selective Trout*, had stressed the red brown color of many mayfly nymphs; so I selected it as the color for this nymph. Bleached guard hairs from the back of a cottontail rabbit proved to be just right for mottled legs. The skin is bleached as recommended by Polly Rosborough. Place a 3 x 3-inch patch of hide in a pint jar and cover it with Miss Clairol Clairoxide. *Do not cap tightly* or the jar may explode. The process takes a couple of days; so watch the fur, and when the soft underfur is a pinkish tan, remove it and rinse for a couple of minutes in cold water. The guard hairs will be dark brown on their tips, pale tan in the midsection, and dark brown again near their bases. They make excellent legs. It was easy to select the pheasant tail fibers for the tail of the nymph, but I couldn't seem to find the right material for the wing case. Nothing looked right. Joe Brooks's book, *Trout Fishing*, had just been published, and as I leafed through it, a color plate showing some of Dave Whitlock's nymphs caught my eye; it wasn't so much the design of the fly as it was the peacock herl wing case. That was the item I'd been looking for. The herl glistened and glinted like the wing pads of a mature nymph. The Red Brown Nymph was complete. It has taken trout on all types of water from Pennsylvania's spring creeks to Montana's big rivers. It is the one nymph I will not be without.

Dressing

Hook:	Sizes 6-18 (especially size 10), Mustad 94840 or 94833
Thread:	Danville prewaxed, dark brown
Tail:	Rusty brown fibers from pheasant tailfeather
Body:	Dark rusty brown dubbing or Mohlon yarn, well picked out; weighted if desired
Legs:	Guard hairs from back of bleached cottontail rabbit pelt
Covert:	Peacock herl

Tying Notes

1. Tie in the tail and weight the body (if desired).
2. Dub on the abdomen, ending at the midpoint of the shank.
3. Tie in a clump of six-eight pieces of peacock herl.
4. Form a dubbing loop and apply dubbing loosely on lower side of loop.
5. Grasp a clump of guard hairs (twenty or so) between your thumb and forefinger and pull them from the hide.

6. Insert the hairs in the loop and at right angles to the thread and spread them along the loop (Fig. A-1).

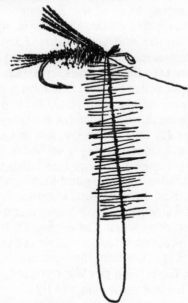

Figure A-1. The Red Brown Nymph, hairs inserted in dubbing loop at right angles to thread.

7. Close the loop and twist it tight, forming a chenille of hair legs.
8. Place a couple of drops of vinyl head cement on the hook shank in the region of the thorax and wind the twisted loop forward, pushing the legs back after each turn to prevent their being wound under. Tie off at the head and cut away the excess.
9. Push the hairs on top of the fly out to the sides. Fold the peacock herl forward tight along the top of the thorax and tie it off at the head. Cut away the excess and finish the head (Fig. A-2).

Figure A-2. The finished Red Brown Nymph.

Variations and Organisms Imitated

In the standard sizes and red brown color, the fly imitates a large number of mayfly nymphs: most of the *Ephemerella*; the *Isonychia* (Large Mahogany Drake); the darker *Stenonema* nymphs; the Quill Gordon *(Epeorus pleuralis)* and some other *Epeorus;* and certain *Siphlonurus*. It also imitates medium-sized stonefly nymphs. I've used it successfully to take trout feeding on scuds, cressbugs, backswimmers, waterboatmen, and adult water beetles. Use hare's mask dubbing and rib the fly with gold tinsel for a beautiful Gold Ribbed Hare's Ear. This version is potent medicine during hatches of the Gray Fox *(Stenonema fuscum)*. On size 10 or 12, 3X long hooks, it's an excellent damselfly imitation if dressed thin. In medium gray it's a fine representation of the Gray Drakes *(Siphlonurus* spp.). In gray it has also worked to imitate scuds. Olive brown dubbing makes a good imitation of some *Epeorus* and *Ephemerella* mayflies. Dark brown, chartreuse, or amber mimic many species of smaller stoneflies. Dark brown and amber versions are excellent for large stoneflies when tied on big 3X long hooks. If the abdomen is ribbed with copper wire and well picked out at the sides, the big amber version works to represent the large burrowing mayflies like *Hexigenia limbata* (the Giant Michigan Mayfly) and *Ephemera simulans* (the Brown Drake). This is a most versatile fly.

HAIR LEG WOOLY WORM

This imitation also evolved from the hair leg experiments. The material used in this nymph was selected for its translucence and movement in the water.

Dressing

Hook:	Sizes 2-18, Mustad 9672, 3X long
Thread:	Monocord, prewaxed, dark brown
Tail:	Clump of black calftail hair, tied short
Abdomen:	Dark brown Mohlon or mohair yarn well picked out at the sides
Rib:	Silver wire on abdomen only
Thorax:	Dark brown Mohlon or mohair yarn, weighted if desired
Legs:	Black calftail hair

Variations and Organisms Imitated

Mohair is my favorite yarn for this fly because it is so easily dyed. Other effective colors include medium brown, olive brown, medium gray, pale orangish gray, and amber. The last two colors are ribbed with bright copper wire rather than silver wire. Fur dubbing can also be used, but keep it coarse. Hare's mask makes an excellent dubbing for this fly. Obviously, the wooly worm larvae are all imitated by this fly. Dark brown, medium brown, and olive brown are most effective for these organisms. In gray, orangish gray, and olive brown, this fly is a good representation of cranefly larvae. Thinly dressed, the pattern has proved effective in matching the damselfly nymphs. Dark brown and amber are good stonefly imitations, especially for the big *Pteronarcys* and *Acroneuria* flies. Sizes 14 and smaller also represent mayfly nymphs, scuds, cressbugs, caddis pupae, large midge pupae, and so on. It's just a good, buggy-looking fly (Fig. A-3).

Figure A-3. The Hair Leg Wooly Worm.

HAIR LEG SCUDS

These were the first flies on which I used the hair leg technique. They've been a standard in my fly box because they so effectively imitate the ubiquitous scuds.

Dressing

Hook:	Sizes 8-16, Mustad 94833 or 94840
Thread:	Danville's prewaxed, light brown
Tail:	End of overlay
Body:	Bleached cottontail rabbit fur from back of pelt, weighted if desired
Rib:	Bright copper wire, 28- to 32-gauge
Overlay:	Wood duck flank or tan-dyed mallard
Legs:	Guard hairs from back of bleached cottontail rabbit pelt

Tying Notes

1. Tie in the overlay at the head, pointing forward over the eye of the hook (Fig. A-4).

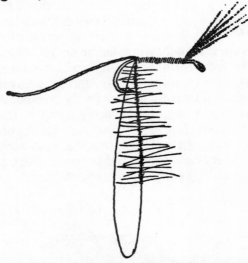

Figure A-4. The Hair Leg Scud with overlay tied in at the head.

2. Form a hair leg chenille at the bend and wrap forward.
3. Push the legs that are sticking out of the top down and to the sides and fold the overlay *back* along the top of the body.
4. Wind the rib forward, securing the overlay in place. Be careful not to wind under too many of the guard hair legs (Fig. A-5).

Figure A-5. The finished Hair Leg Scud.

Variations and Organisms Imitated

A scud is a scud is a scud, and this fly is strictly a scud imitation. But scuds are so widespread in our trout streams and their body plan so strikingly different from other organisms that they deserve a pattern all their own. The pinkish tan color ribbed with copper wire and gray and olive ribbed with silver wire will cover most waters.

Cressbugs are close relatives of the scuds and locally important as trout fodder. A *coarsely* dubbed body spun on a dubbing loop and trimmed flat on the bottom with an overlay of wood duck or dyed mallard and ribbed with wire is a fine imitation.

THE MONO STONEFLY NYMPH

George Grant of Butte, Montana, is an innovative and highly skilled fly tier. His creations should be framed rather than fished. Influenced by the writings of Ed Hewitt and Paul Young, Grant developed his semiflat "creeper" body around 1931. It is the best I've seen for imitating the pronounced segmentation and smooth translucence of the stonefly's abdomen. He describes his tying techniques in *The Art of Weaving Hair Hackles for Trout Flies*.

The pattern given below is for the Mono Salmon Fly Nymph.

Dressing

Hook:	Sizes 2-6, Mustad 9672, 3X long
Thread:	Monocord, prewaxed, black
Tail:	Quill from short side of goose primary wingfeather, dyed black
Foundation:	Lead-core trolling line or lead fuse wire tied in at sides; additional weight may be added by first wrapping the shank with lead wire
Underbody:	Pink floss, lacquered with head cement, colored black on top with waterproof marker or enamel
Abdomen:	Flat monofilament dyed gray
Thorax:	Black-and-white dubbing applied coarsely in clumps on a dubbing loop and well picked out; the white fur will represent the quills
Legs:	Black calftail hair
Wing Cases:	Dark turkey, lacquered with vinyl head cement
Antennae:	Optional; if preferred, dark turkey fibers

Tying Notes

1. Form a small knob of thread at the bend.
2. Tie a goose quill on either side of the shank and wrap back against the knob to spread the tails.

3. Cut the lead-core line to a chisel point (use fingernail clippers). Lay it along one side of the shank such that the tapered end is a short ways ahead of the thread knob. Wrap the thread forward to about the center of the thorax.
4. Fold the lead-core line over the top of the shank and press it flat against the other side. Using the fingernail clippers, snip off the line to form a chisel point opposite the first end. Wrap the thread back to the bend (Fig. A-6).

Figure A-6. The Mono Stonefly Nymph with tails and foundation in place.

5. Wrap the floss along the entire shank to form a smooth under-body. Wrap the mono forward and tie off at the midpoint of the shank. The section of dark turkey fibers should be about 1½ times as wide as the abdomen and tied in tip first at the rear of the thorax.
6. Wrap the leg chenille a turn or two forward and tie off. *Do not cut off the excess.*
7. Hold the turkey feather segment back along the abdomen and crimp it with your thumbnail a short ways behind the thorax. Fold it forward over the thorax and tie down in front of the legs to form the rear wing pads (Fig. A-7).
8. Repeat to form the front half of the thorax (Fig. A-8).

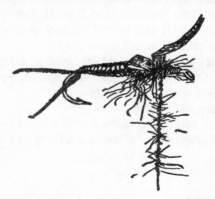

Figure A-7. The Mono Stonefly Nymph, showing folding of wing pads.

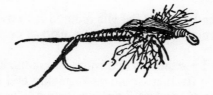

Figure A-8. The finished Mono Stonefly Nymph.

Variations and Organisms Imitated

Stonefly nymphs are common inhabitants of fast water and gravel bottoms throughout the United States. Many of the nymphs live for more than a year, and the trout are well acquainted with them, feeding on them all year long. Below is a list of the most used sizes and colors of the big Mono Stonefly Nymphs; E=East, M=Midwest, W=West.

Dark Mono Stonefly Nymph—imitates the Giant Black Stonefly (*Pteronarcys dorsata*) (E, M) and the Black Willow Fly (*Acroneuria nigrita*) (W). Sizes 2-10, Mustad 9672; black goose quill tail; black or dark brown floss underbody; white and black thorax; black calftail hair legs; and dark turkey wing pads.

Amber Mono Stonefly Nymph—imitates many species in the family Perlidae (E, M, W). Sizes 6-10, Mustad 9672; orange brown goose quill tail; underbody of amber or gold floss mottled on top with brown felt tip pen; orange brown and white dubbing for thorax; legs of bleached rabbit guard hairs; light mottled turkey, dyed with yellow brown, waterproof pen for wing pads.

The pattern given for the Mono Salmon Fly Nymph may also be tied with a yellow or orange underbody colored black on top to imitate other large species of the family Perlidae (E, M, W). Hook sizes are 6-10, Mustad 9672.

MONO CADDIS LARVA

Uncased caddis larvae are more plentiful than many people suppose. In the Midwest they are the single most abundant insect in trout streams. Many anglers imitate these larvae with dubbed fur bodies and a soft hackle; Rosborough's Green Rock Worm is a good example. This pattern represents the free-living, green larva of the *Rhyacophila* caddis. The abdomen is medium to dark green, the legs are green dyed guinea fibers, the head is black ostrich herl. Ernie Schwiebert recommends similar patterns in *Nymphs*. Ral Boaze of Brunswick, Maryland, developed the latex caddis. His method is to overwind a floss or yarn abdomen with a ⅛- to ¼-inch-wide strip of cream-colored sheet latex.

The pattern that I use most is tied with a flat mono abdomen. It came from the need for a fly that would sink quickly and stay down in the riffles where larvae of the Net Spinning Caddis (Hydropsychidae) and the Green Rock Worm dwell. George Grant's persuasive arguments for flat nylon-bodied nymphs led me to experiment with the material. The Mono Caddis Larva has proved to be a fine imitation.

Dressing

Hook:	Sizes 8-14, Mustad 94833 or 94840; for a more curved body, Mustad 37160 can be used
Thread:	Danville's prewaxed, gray
Underbody:	Gray floss, weighted if desired
Abdomen:	Flat mono (12-lb. test), dyed pale gray
Rib:	Tying thread
Gills:	Ostrich herl secured against underside of abdomen
Thorax:	Black dubbing
Legs:	Black calftail hair

Tying Notes

1. Leave the waste end of the tying thread for the rib.
2. Tie in the herl on the underside of the thorax and pointing back under the abdomen. Wrap the rib forward to secure the herl against the underside of the mono abdomen (Fig. A-9).

Figure A-9. The Mono Caddis Larva, gilled version.

Variations and Organisms Imitated

I use this fly to imitate caddis larvae, but the trout may think it's something else such as a cranefly larva or scud. I really don't care. The dressing I've shown above is for the gray larva of the Net Spinning Caddis. Other colors for the abdomen are dirty white, gray olive, dirty olive yellow, and green. The Green Rock Worm larva can be imitated in this fashion, but the gills are omitted.

MUSKRAT NYMPH

The simplicity of this fly is in itself a virtue, but it's the effectiveness of the Muskrat year in and year out that makes it a mandatory requirement for a fully stocked nymph box (Fig. A-10).

Figure A-10. The Muskrat Nymph.

Dressing

Hook:	Sizes 2-20, Mustad 94833 or 94840
Thread:	Monocord, prewaxed, on larger sizes; Danville's prewaxed on smaller sizes; gray
Tail:	Clump of fibers from coot feather
Body:	Blend of 1 part muskrat fur, 1 part cottontail rabbit fur, 1 part gray squirrel fur, ⅛ part black dyed rabbit fur; leave in the guard hairs and spin fur on dubbing loop for coarse appearance; weighted if desired
Hackle:	Body feather from lower neck region of coot.

Variations and Organisms Imitated

You can tie this basic tail/body/hackle pattern in any color you can imagine. But, fo: variations on the nymph theme, I use dark brown, gray brown, olive brown, red brown, and pinkish tan. These colors are generally imitative of the whole range of aquatic food organisms. A very interesting modification of the basic Muskrat is a fly developed by Lacey Gee and called the Gimp. For this fly, a wing of filoplume feather is added before the hackle is wound on. The filoplume is a small maraboulike feather on the underside of the body feather of game birds like grouse, quail, and pheasant. It is a nice, deep, blue-gray color. If you bleach a piece of pheasant hide in Clairoxide, the filoplumes will turn tan. As such, they make excellent wings for the tan version of the muskrat. These bleached feathers can also be dyed to other shades. I'm convinced that the maraboulike undulations of the filoplume simulate gills or give the entire fly the look of a swimming nymph. It's not necessary to use coot feathers on the Muskrat, or an exotic blend of furs for that matter, but over the years I've come to prize the gun metal blue of the coot and the heather mix of fur. They make a most appealing fly.

STRIP NYMPH

Royce Dam is a custom fly tier from Franklin, Wisconsin, and a good one, too. Several years ago we were discussing the Tomorrow River, and he showed me a fly that he'd used quite successfully there. The wing on the fly was unique; it was a narrow strip of muskrat hide with the fur intact. "It has all the advantages of marabou," Royce told me, "but it's tougher." I especially like this tying method for the big burrowing mayfly nymphs.

Dressing

Hook:	Sizes 6-10, Mustad 94833 or 94840
Thread:	Monocord, prewaxed, tan
Abdomen:	Strip of tanned muskrat hide with fur on, bleached to tan color.
Wing Case:	Peacock herl
Thorax:	Tan fur, dubbed coarse
Legs:	Bleached cottontail rabbit guard hairs

Tying Notes

1. Use a ⅛-inch-wide strip from the tanned hide and tie it in as a tail. It should be slightly longer than the hook shank; it will form the abdomen of the fly.
2. Weight the thorax with lead wire.
3. Spin some dubbing on the thread and wind over the rear ¼ of the hook shank.
4. Finish as for the Red Brown Nymph (Fig. A-11).

Figure A-11. The Strip Nymph.

Variations and Organisms Imitated

The weighted thorax on this fly increases the undulations of the abdomen when the fly is fished with a jigging motion. *Hexigenia* nymphs are good swimmers, rising from their burrows in the firm silt bottoms and wiggling to the surface to hatch. Any of the larger burrowing mayfly nymphs is well imitated by this pattern: nymphs of *Hexigenia*, *Ephemera*, *Potamanthus*, and *Epheron*. Short-furred pelts such as mole can be used to tie smaller Strip Nymphs to imitate the medium-sized mayflies.

This fly also makes the best leech imitation I've ever used. The tail is red marabou tied short; the body is coarsely dubbed gray fur, weighted; the wing is a long strip of muskrat fur tied in at the head and ribbed against the body, Matuka style. In lakes, this fly is very effective when fished with the strip/tease technique.

THE WET/DRY FLY

Dressing

Hook:	Sizes 12-18, Mustad 94833; sizes 20-24, Mustad 94842 (turned-up eye)
Thread:	Danville's prewaxed, color to match body
Tail:	None
Body:	Dubbed fur
Hackle:	Covert feather (Fig. A-12)

Figure A-12. The Wet/Dry Fly.

Variations and Organisms Imitated

The hackle is the key to this fly. It must be taken from the shoulder of the wing (covert feathers). These feathers have wide, soft barbs unlike the thin barbs of body feathers. The wide fiber gives necessary body to the fly, simulating crumpled wings and legs. In addition, it is much better for floating the fly. On hooks size 14 and larger, use two hackles. For light gray hackle use mallard or snipe; for slate gray, coot;

for the browns, grouse and woodcock; for the creams, pheasant. The most widely used colors (wing/body) and sizes are: slate/olive, 12-20; slate/gray, 12-24; gray/sulphur, 14-24; slate/rusty brown, 12-20; brown/tan, 12-20; gray/black, 20-24; cream/tan, 12-24. This range of colors will imitate many of the mayflies, midges, and caddises. Other colors can be added if you find them locally important.

SAWYER'S PHEASANT TAIL

I was given Frank Sawyer's *Nymphs and the Trout* for my birthday in 1973. I was impressed by his thoroughness, but it was the simplicity of his nymphs that captivated my attention. I simply couldn't get them out of my mind, especially the Pheasant Tail or "p.t." as he called it. That summer's Montana trip included a day on the little-known spring creek, and in 2 hours, the p.t. took 27 fish between 1 and 3½ pounds. I'd only covered 100 feet of the stream as the hatch of Pale Morning Duns (*Ephemerella infrequens*) ended. That was the first of many such experiences.

Dressing

Hook:	Sizes 14-20, Mustad 94833 or 94840
Thread:	Danville's prewaxed, dark brown
Tail:	Tips of fibers used to form body
Body:	Rusty brown, well-mottled fibers from pheasant tail feather with dark center stripe on backside, weighted
Covert:	Butt ends of fibers used for body, folded and secured on top of thorax

Tying Notes

1. Tie in the pheasant fibers so that their tips form the tail of the fly.
2. Twist the tying thread and fibers together lightly. The thread will reinforce the body.
3. Wind the twisted fibers forward to the head and tie off, but *do not* cut away the excess.
4. Fold the butt ends of the fibers back over the thorax and wrap the thread over them in an open spiral to hold them in place. Wrap just to the rear of the thorax. Now wrap forward to the head, fold

the butt ends forward, and secure them with the thread. Repeat if there's enough fiber left. Try to get enough folds so that the wing case is prominently bulging on the back of the thorax (Fig. A-13).

Figure A-13. Sawyer's p.t.

Variations and Organisms Imitated

In rusty brown, the p.t. imitates the little nymphs of *Ephemerella*, the *Paraleptophlebia*, and some *Baetis* and *Callibaetis*. By using olive or olive yellow dyed pheasant tail, the fly will simulate many other small mayfly nymphs.

SOUTH PLATTE BRASSY

Above Deckers, the tumbling South Platte forces its tortuous way through the Front Range, forming a blend of runs, pools, riffles, and rapids among room-sized boulders. Regulars on the river have developed a unique collection of nymphs for the picky rainbows and browns—flies like the South Platte Brassy. I first saw the Brassy described by Ed Marsh in the April, 1971, issue of *Field and Stream*. He gave credit to Gene Lynch of Colorado Springs for originating the fly. I've taken many fine trout on the Brassy; it is one of my favorite spring creek flies.

Dressing

Hook:	Sizes 14-20, Mustad 94833 or 94840
Thread:	Danville's prewaxed, fluorescent red
Body:	Bright copper wire; 24-gauge for size 14, 26-gauge for size 16 and 18, 28-gauge for size 20
Throat:	Pheasant tail fibers (Fig. A-14)

Figure A-14. South Platte Brassy.

Variations and Organisms Imitated

I am convinced this bare bones fly represents the brownish to blood-red larvae of many Chironomidae midges. These insects are widespread and abundant in trout streams, especially weedy areas in spring creeks. The original pattern was tied with black thread and had black fur at the throat. The body was built up with thread or floss into a cigar shape before the wire was wound on. This thicker version is a decent look-alike for the tan scuds.

MIDGE PUPA

There are many rather elaborate pupa patterns, but I prefer the simple ones. They're easiest to tie and just as deadly as the more complicated patterns. The simplest of them all is the one Ed Koch shows in *Fishing the Midge;* he calls it the Midge Nymph.

Dressing

Hook:	Sizes 14-18, Mustad 94833 or 94840; sizes 20-28, Mustad 94842
Thread:	Danville's prewaxed, color to match body
Body:	Dubbed fur, coarse, weighted if desired (Fig. A-15)

Figure A-15. Midge Nymph.

Variations and Organisms Imitated

This is such an easy fly to tie that it almost seems like cheating to use it. Yet, it is an effective addition to any nymph box. I've found gray, gray brown, olive brown, and rusty brown to be the most used colors. The dubbing I like for these little flies is a blend of short, medium, and long hairs. For the gray ones, I use the same blend as for the Muskrat Nymph. Such blends give the finished fly a rough look. The hairs poking out at various angles greatly enhance the impression of life so vital to successful imitations. Besides the midge pupae, this little nymph will imitate small mayfly nymphs and larvae of caddises, beetles, and moths.

Another midge pupa worth describing is the one given in *Selective Trout*. The abdomen is thinly dubbed fur of appropriate color; the thorax is dark brown or black and dubbed full (Fig. A-16). Ed Koch

Figure A-16. Caddis Midge.

also describes this fly, calling it the Caddis Midge since it imitates the pupae of microcaddises so well.

GRIFFITH'S GNAT

Ernie Schwiebert's *Nymphs* is a book of startling magnitude, rich in angling lore and immensely detailed with information on aquatic food organisms of the trout. During my first reading of the book, I was taken by his description of Griffith's Gnat and its use as an emerger pattern for midges. The fly and the situations described for its use filled a gap in my midge fishing. Again, as I have so often found, the simple fly meets a complex need.

Dressing

Hook:	Sizes 14-18, Mustad 94833 or 94840; sizes 20-24, Mustad 94842
Thread:	Danville's prewaxed, black
Body:	Peacock herl
Hackle:	Grizzly, palmered (Fig. A-17)

Figure A 17 Griffith s Gnat

Variations and Organisms Imitated

The dressing given above is the original, and it's extremely effective when the black or gray midges are emerging. Schwiebert mentions a host of other colors for the body, substituting floss for the herl. I prefer dubbing and have found gray, black, rusty brown, olive brown, pale yellow, and pale green to be the most used colors. Grizzly hackle works well on all these patterns; blue dun and brown are also effective. The hackle creates a light diffraction pattern in the film which gives the impression of a partially cast pupal husk. Schwiebert mentions trimming the hackle top and bottom to get a flush float for picky trout. It's good advice. These files can also be fished just under the film, either dead drift or with an occasional twitch.

Appendix B

KEYS TO SUBAQUATIC FOOD ORGANISMS OF THE TROUT

It is beyond the scope of this book to build keys to every subaquatic, invertebrate organism, if in fact that's possible, but the organisms described are those most important to the fly fisher. These keys have been built as much as possible on easily seen and recognized characteristics such as number of tails, body size, color, and so on. Organisms are keyed to order with further keys, in most cases, to family, occasionally to genus, rarely to species. The keys to orders are dichotomous, offering a yes/no choice for each characteristic. For example, if the organism does not possess the characteristics in 1a, then the choice is 1b. A number following the choice directs you to the next set of choices. Other keys may be dichotomous or may simply list the major characteristics of each group.

There are four angling texts that can be of further help in identifying the subaquatic food organisms of the trout. Ernest Schwiebert's *Nymphs* is a book of encyclopedic proportions with innumerable details and superb drawings of aquatic forms. It is a reference text all serious nymph fishers should have. Al Caucci and Bob Nastasi's *Hatches* is a fine text on the mayflies with sound descriptions and excellent photographs. Caddises are well treated in Larry Solomon and Eric Leiser's excellent text, *The Caddis and The Angler*. Al McClane's *New Standard Fishing Encyclopedia and International Angling Guide* has good keys to mayflies and stoneflies. Some valuable scientific treatises are listed in a special reference section at the end of this book.

The only special piece of equipment needed for identifying insects is a 10 or 20X hand lens.

Phylum Arthropoda, class Crustacea

Three orders within this class are important to the angler. The Decapoda are crayfish, the Amphipoda are the scuds (Fig. B-1), and the Isopoda are the cressbugs (Fig. B-2).

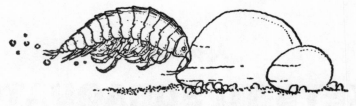

Figure B-1. A typical scud.

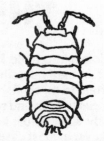

Figure B-2. A cressbug.

Phylum Mollusca

The class Gastropoda contains the snails which often serve as trout food.

Phylum Annelida

Within the class Oligochaeta there are a number of truly aquatic earthworms. Some trout streams have abundant populations of these creatures. Leeches are found in the class Hirudinea; they are widespread and readily taken by trout.

Phylum Arthropoda, class Insecta

Insects may have one of three life cycles. The angler should understand the differences, both as an aid to identification and to selecting the correct nymphing tactic. In the *complete* cycle there's an egg, a larva (soft body and wormlike), a pupa (transforming stage), and adult. Insect orders with a complete cycle are the Trichoptera, Diptera, Megaloptera, Coleoptera, and Lepidoptera. The *incomplete* cycle has an egg, a nymph (correctly, a naiad; it does not look like the adult), and an adult. The orders Emphemeroptera, Plecoptera, and Odonata have an incomplete cycle. A *gradual* cycle is characterized by an egg, a nymph (looks like a small adult and gradually grows larger), and an adult. The order Hemiptera has this type of life cycle.

KEY TO ORDERS OF INSECTS

1a. Thorax with 3 pairs of *jointed* legs (Fig. B-16) . . . 3
1b. Thorax without jointed legs (Fig. B-11) . . . 2

    2a Rather indistinct body form enclosed in definite sealed case: various pupae (not keyed)
    2b. Motile larva not in case, body fleshy; if legs present, they are *not* jointed (Fig. B-7, B-9): order Diptera

3a. Wing pads present (Fig. B-15) . . . 4
3b. Wing pads absent (Fig. B-12) . . . 8

    4a. Insect with 2 or 3, long, slender, filamentous tails (Fig. B-15) . . . 5
    4b. Insect without tails *or* tails paddle-shaped . . . 6

5a. Gills on upper surface or at sides of abdomen, only one pair of wing pads visible (Fig. B-15, B-26): order Ephemeroptera
5b. Gills threadlike, in clusters, and occurring near base of legs; *or* gills lacking, two pairs of wing pads visible: order Plecoptera

    6a. Tails paddle-shaped, insect body long and rangy, legs long, eyes large (Fig. B-38): suborder Zygoptera, order Odonata
    6b. Tails absent . . . 7

7a. Mouthparts broadly triangular or modified into a tube for sucking; wings if present, with only forepart thickened; middle leg with two claws, other legs with one claw (Fig. B-33): order Hemiptera
7b. Mouthparts jointed to form an extending, grasping structure, body broad and flattened, eyes large (Fig. B-37): suborder Anisoptera, order Odonata

    8a. Mouthparts broadly triangular or formed into a tube for sucking, walking on water's surface, or swimming, middle leg with two claws: order Hemiptera
    8b. Mouthparts not formed into tube, body wormlike, abdomen soft (Figs. B-11, B-44) . . . 9

9a. Insect with fleshy, lobelike prolegs (similar to those of caterpillar) on bottom side of abdominal segments: order Lepidoptera
9b. Prolegs absent from bottom side of abdominal segments with possible exception of last segment . . . 10

    10a. Antennae inconspicuous; insect often in case of twigs, pebbles, etc.; some species not in case: order Trichoptera. *Note:*

if insect without case, gills lacking from the underside of its abdomen, and abdominal segments strongly angled on upper side (Fig. B-4), see key to Coleoptera

10b. Antennae short but readily visible . . . 11

11a. One claw on each leg: order Coleoptera

11b. Two claws on each leg . . . 12

12a. Filaments lacking on abdomen: order Coleoptera

12b. Conspicuous filaments on sides of abdomen (Fig. B-36) . . . 13

13a. Abdomen ending in two slender filaments *or* 1 median lobe having 4 hooks: order Coleoptera

13b. Abdomen ending with 1 slender, featherlike filament *or* in 2 lobes each with 2 hooks (Figs. B-34, B-35): order Megaloptera

KEY TO LARVAE OF COLEOPTERA, beetles (*coleo*, sheath; *ptera*, wing: referring to the thickened forewing or elytra)

1a. Legs with 2 claws each . . . 2

1b. Legs with 1 claw each . . . 3

2a. Abdomen ending in four conspicuous hooks, at least 8 pairs of lateral filaments on the abdomen: family Gyrinidae

2b. Abdomen lacking hooks, only 6 pairs or fewer lateral filaments on abdomen, abdomen tapering rearward; family Dytiscidae

3a. Abdomen ending in one or two taillike filaments: family Haliplidae

3b. Abdomen not ending in long filaments . . . 4

4a. Mandibles large and easily seen from above (Fig. B-3): family Hydrophilidae

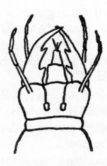

Figure B-3. Head of Hydrophilidae beetle larva.

4b. Mandibles inconspicuous from above, abdomen strongly segmented, segments very angular on upper side (Fig. B-4): family Elmidae

Figure B-4. Elmidae beetle larva.

KEY TO LARVAE OF DIPTERA, mosquitoes, midges, and craneflies (*di,* two; *ptera,* wing: referring to adults which have only two wings)
1. Larva of glasslike transparency with a dark air sac at each end, about 13 mm long (Fig. B-5): family Chaoboridae, phantom midges; springs and lakes

Figure B-5. Chaoboridae larva.

2. Larva 7-segmented with sucker on bottom of each of first 6 segments (Fig. B-6): family Blephariceridae, genus *Blepharicera,* net-winged midges; fast rocky streams

Figure B-6. *Blepharicera* larva.

3. Abdomen with 7 pairs of fleshy, lobelike prolegs along the sides (Fig B-7): family Deuterophlebiidae, genus *Deuterophlebia*, mountain midges; clear, rocky, mountain streams

Figure B-7. *Deuterophlebia* larva.

4. Abdomen ending in respiratory disk, head retractable into body, mouthparts closing horizontally; often large insects (to 60 mm or more) (Fig. B-8): family Tipulidae, craneflies; streams and lakes

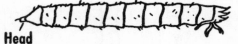

Head

Figure B-8. Tipulidae larva.

5. Last third of abdomen swollen and terminating in a disk used to attach larva to bottom, usually 5 mm long or less (Fig. B-9): family Simulidae, black flies or buffalo gnats; shallow swift water

Figure B-9. Simulidae larva.

6. Larva pointed on both ends, body ringed with swollen, fleshy prolegs (Fig. B-10): family Tabanidae, horseflies (lakes) and deerflies (streams)

Figure B-10. Tabanidae larva.

7. Body thin and wormlike, prolegs on first thoracic segment and last abdominal segment (Fig. B-11): family Chironomidae, midges; lakes and streams

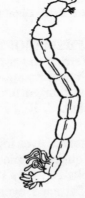

Figure B-11. Chironomidae larva.

8. Thorax segments fused and larger in diameter than rest of body (Fig. B-12): family Culicidae, mosquitoes; lakes and streams

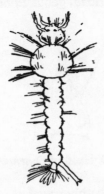

Figure B-12. Culicidae larva.

9. Thorax segments not fused, body nearly same diameter throughout, larva takes on definite U-shape at rest (Fig. B-13): family **Dixidae**, dixa midges; lakes and slow water areas in streams

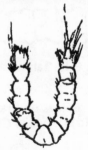

Figure B-13. Dixidae larva.

KEY TO NYMPHS OF EPHEMEROPTERA, mayflies (*ephemero*, short-lived; *ptera*, wing: referring to short life of adult)

1a. Abdomen soft and fleshy, often tan-colored, gills very large and feathery, legs broad and flanged for digging, tusks present (Fig. B-15): burrowing nymphs . . . **Key I**

1b. Not as above . . . 2

    2a. Body strongly flattened, eyes located entirely on top of head, gills platelike and quite conspicuous on abdominal segments 1-7: clinging nymphs . . . **Key II** (family Heptageniidae)

    2b. Body not strongly flattened, eyes located at sides of head, gills variable: swimming and crawling nymphs . . . **Key III**

KEY I, BURROWING NYMPHS; soft body, feathery gills, tusks

1a. Frontal prominence extended and notched, tusks outcurved (Fig. B-14): family Ephermeridae, genus *Ephemera*

Figure B-14. Head of *Ephemera* nymph.

1b. Frontal prominence smoothly rounded . . . 2

2a. Tusks upcurved, very large nymph burrowing in silt (Fig.
B-15): family Ephemeridae, genus *Hexigenia*

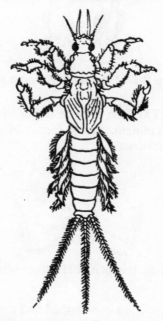

Figure B-15. *Hexigenia* nymph.

2b. Tusks not as above . . . 3

3a. Tusks distinctly hornlike, legs broadly flattened, in gravel (Fig.
B-16): family Potamanthidae, genus *Potamanthus*

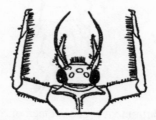

Figure B-16. Forepart of *Potamanthus* nymph.

3b. Tusks incurved with many bumps and hairs, frontal prominence
slightly extended (Fig. B-17): family Polymitarcidae, genus *Epho-*
ron

Figure B-17. Forepart of *Ephoron* nymph.

KEY II, CLINGING NYMPHS; eyes on top of head (Fig. B-18), body strongly flattened, gills platelike; all in family Heptageniidae
1a. Two tails: genus *Epeorus*
1b. Three tails . . . 2

Figure B-18. Forepart of Heptageniidae nymph.

2a. Gills 1 and 7 suction cup-shaped and much larger than other gills (Fig. B-19): genus *Rithrogena*
2b. Gills 1 and 7 not modified as above . . . 3

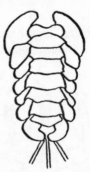

Figure B-19. Bottom view of abdomen of *Rithrogena* nymph.

3a. Seventh gill threadlike, 1-6 platelike, tails widely spread and quite rigid: genus *Stenonema*
3b. Appearance similar to *Stenonema*, but seventh gill distinctly platelike: genus *Heptagenia*

KEY III, CRAWLING AND SWIMMING NYMPHS

1a. Nymph with 2 tails, small insect 3-6 mm (Fig. B-20): family Baetidae, genus *Pseudocloeon*

Figure B-20. *Pseudocloeon* nymph

1b. Nymph with 3 tails . . . 2

    2a. Top of thorax greatly enlarged into prominent hump that extends back over first 5 segments of the abdomen (Fig. B-21): family Baetiscidae, genus *Baetisca*

Figure B-21. *Baetisca* nymph.

    2b. Top of thorax not enlarged . . . 3

3a. Nymph with 3 tails of equal length . . . 4

3b. Nymph with 3 tails, center tail distinctly shorter than outer tails, tails heavily fringed, slender head tilted downward, gill plates single, gills on abdominal segments 1-7, nymphs 4-10 mm (Fig. B-22): family Baetidae, genus *Baetis*

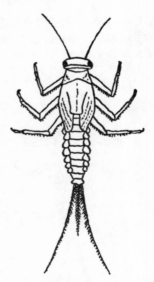

Figure B-22. *Baetis* nymph.

     4a. Nymphs small, 2-7 mm, average 3-4 mm, first gill enlarged to cover remaining gills . . . 5

     4b. All gills visible, first gill not enlarged to cover other gills . . . 7

5a. First gill triangular in outline (Fig. B-23): family Tricorythidae, genus *Tricorythodes*

Figure B-23. First gill of *Tricorythodes* nymph.

5b. First gill nearly rectangular in outline (Fig. B-24): family Caenidae . . . 6

Figure B-24. First gill of Caenidae nymph.

6a. Head with 3 prominent hornlike projections (Fig. B-25): genus *Brachycerus*

Figure B-25. Head of *Brachycerus* nymph.

6b. Head without prominent hornlike projections: genus *Caenis*

7a. Gills on abdominal segments 3-7 or 4-7 only, platelike, wider than long; spines well developed at sides of abdomen (Fig. B-26): family Ephemerellidae, genus *Ephemerella*

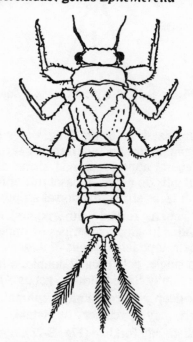

Figure B-26. An *Ephemerella* nymph.

7b. Gills occurring on abdominal segments 1-7 . . . 8

    8a. Gills single (in some species the first 2 gills may be double, but the rest are singular) . . . 9

    8b. All gills double; both parts may be similar in shape *or* one may be platelike the other bushy *or* one may be smaller than the other . . . 11

9a. Small nymphs, 3-6 mm long, gills platelike (Fig. B-27): family Baetidae, genus *Cloeon* (also *Centroptilium*, which occurs rarely in spring creeks)

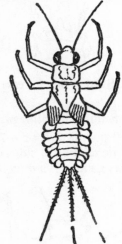

Figure B-27. A typical *Cloeon* nymph.

9b. Nymph medium-sized, 6-16 mm long, outer rear edge of each abdominal segment drawn out into a sharp, flattened spine (nymph has general appearance and shape of genus *Isonychia* (Fig. B-32), but gills do not have basal tuft of feathery secondary gills and nymph lacks strong middorsal stripe) . . . 10

    10a. Claw on front leg forked (with 2 points), other claws single; nymph with 3 longitudinal stripes on underside of abdomen: family Metretopodidae, genus *Siphloplecton*

    10b. All claws single, gills 1 and 2 double, others single, all gills platelike: family Siphlonuridae, genus *Siphlonurus*

11a. Gills forked or deeply lobed: family Leptophlebiidae . . . 12

11b. Gills not forked, may be feathery or platelike . . . 13

    12a. All gills distinctly forklike (Fig. B-28), nymphs 6-8 mm long, head squarish: genus *Paraleptophlebia*

Figure B-28. Forked gill of *Paraleptophlebia* nymph.

12b. Gills on first abdominal segment forklike, all other gills lobed (Fig. B-29); nymphs 10-14 mm long: genus *Leptophlebia*

Figure B-29. Lobed gill of *Leptophlebia* nymph.

13a. Gills double and ovate, secondary gill smaller (Fig. B-30); **nymph often with dark band on apical end of tails: family Baetidae, genus** *Callibaetis*

Figure B-30. Gill of *Callibaetis* nymph.

13b. Gills double, secondary gill tuftlike (Fig. B-31), tails heavily fringed, forelegs heavily fringed, body of equal width from head to tail, strong middorsal stripe present (Fig. B-32): family Siphlonuridae, genus *Isonychia*

Figure B-31. Gill of *Isonychia* nymph.

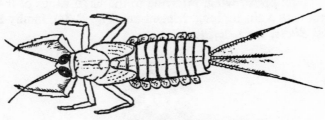

Figure B-32. *Isonychia* nymph.

KEY TO ADULT HEMIPTERA, true bugs (*hemi*, half; *ptera*, wing: referring to forewings, which are thickened on basal half)

1. Beak broad, blunt, and triangular, tarus (T) of front leg a one-segmented scoop (Fig. B-33): family Corixidae, waterboatmen; pond dwellers, widespread in lakes and streams, they fly to large rivers and lakes to overwinter

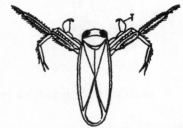

Figure B-33. An adult Corixidae. T=tarsus.

2. Beak cylindrical, tarsus of foreleg not a scoop and with several segments, large insects (over 18 mm, usually much larger): family Belostomatidae, giant water bugs; fierce predators that live in ponds and lakes, they fly to streams to overwinter
3. Beak cylindrical, tarsus of foreleg not a scoop and with several segments, insect less than 16 mm long, body flattened, insect swims upside down: family Notonectidae, backswimmers; live in ponds and lakes with emergent vegetation; predators, they disperse widely

Order LEPIDOPTERA, aquatic moths (*Lepido*, scale; *ptera*, wing: referring to the scales on the wings)

All aquatic moths are in the family Pyralidae. Most genera live in ponds and build cases of plant material. One genus, *Paraqyractis*, lives in fast-water areas of streams. It has about 120 unbranched gill filaments on the abdomen.

KEY TO LARVAE OF MEGALOPTERA, dobsonfly, fish fly, alderfly (*megalo*, large; *ptera*, wing: referring to the large wings of the adult)
1a. Insect with a single, long, fringed tail (Fig. B-34): family Sialidae, genus *Sialis*, the alderflies

Figure B-34. End of abdomen of *Sialis* larva.

1b. Insect with two terminal lobes, each with two hooks (Fig. B-35): family Corydalidae . . . 2

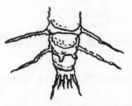

Figure B-35. End of abdomen of *Nigronia* larva.

2a. Each lateral abdominal filament with large tuft of threadlike gills at base, mature larva large (to 90 mm) and pugnacious: *Corydalus cornutus*, the hellgrammite (dobsonfly larva) (Fig. B-36)

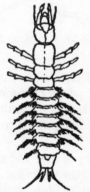

Figure B-36. Larva of *Corydalus cornutus*.

2b. Tufts of threadlike gills lacking: fishflies . . . 3

3a. Respiratory tubes on top of abdominal segment 8 short, not extending beyond middle of segment 9 (Fig. B-35): genus *Nigronia*, black fishfly

3b. Respiratory tubes extending past end of abdomen: genus *Chauliodes*, tan fishfly

Order ODONATA, dragonflies and damselflies (*odus*, a tooth: referring to the large mandibles)

Most species dwell in calm waters, but dragonflies of the families Gomphidae and Cordulegastridae inhabit riffles. In the Gomphidae the labium (L) folds back flat under the head (Fig. B-37), whereas in the Cordulegastridae the labium forms a mask over the front of the head and extends upward as far as the base of the antennae.

Figure B-37. Extendable labium (*L*) of Odonate nymph.

Both dragonflies and damselflies have extendable, hinged mouthparts (Fig. B-37). Damselflies (suborder Zygoptera) are easily recognized by their 3 paddle-shaped tails and thin body (Fig. B-38). Dragonflies (suborder Anisoptera) lack tails and have a wide, flattened abdomen.

Figure B-38. A typical damselfly.

KEY TO NYMPHS OF PLECOPTERA, stoneflies (*pleco*, pleat; *ptera*, wing: referring to the folded wings of the resting adult)
1a. Branched, threadlike gills on underside of entire thorax . . . 2
1b. Gills not branched *or* gills confined to first segment of thorax *or* gills absent . . . 3
    2a. Gills also on bottom of first and second abdominal segments (Fig. B-39): family Pteronarcidae, genus *Pteronarcys*, largest North American stoneflies, includes salmon fly and giant black stonefly; emerge late spring to midsummer

Figure B-39. Gills of *Pteronarcys nymph*. *T*=thorax, *A*=abdomen.

    2b. Gills confined to thorax: family Perlidae, includes many large species such as the willow fly and amber stonefly of genera *Acroneuria*, *Paragnetina*, *Perlesta*, and others; emerge all summer

3a. Body roachlike in appearance, plates on underside of thorax forming an extension that overlaps the segment behind, family Peltoperlidae, genus *Peltoperla;* found in cold mountain streams; emerge in summer

3b. Body not roachlike, plates on underside of thorax not overlapping . . . 4

    4a. Paraglossae and glossae of mouthparts about equal length (look at underside of head) (Fig. B-40) . . . 5

    4b. Paraglossae extending well beyond glossae (Fig. B-41) . . . 8

Figure B-40. Paraglossae (*P*) and glossae (*G*) equal in length.

Figure B-41. Paraglossae (*P*) extending well beyond glossae (*G*).

5a. Second segment of tarsus as long or longer than first segment (Fig. B-42): family Taeniopterygidae, includes early brown stonefly; emerge in early spring

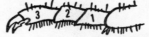

Figure B-42. Tarsus of Taeniopterygidae nymph showing second segment as long as first.

5b. Second segment of tarsus much shorter than first segment . . . 6

    6a. Hind wing pads flared strongly outward from body, nymphs stout: family Nemouridae, genus *Nemoura;* emerge in spring

    6b. Hind wing pads parallel with body, nymphs elongate and slender . . . 7

7a. Top and bottom of segments 1-9 of abdomen separated by a membrane fold (Fig. B-43): family Capniidae, includes genera *Capnia* and *Isocapnia;* emerge in winter

Figure B-43. Abdomen of Capniidae nymph.

7b. Membranous fold occurring at most on first 7 abdominal segments: family Leuctridae, needleflies; emerge in early spring

    8a. Body distinctly patterned, often bright yellow-colored, tails equal in length to or longer than the abdomen, simple gills may be present: family Perlodidae; emerge in midsummer

    8b. Body almost uniformly colored, tails not more than ¾ as long as abdomen, gills never present: family Chloroperlidae, many species yellow, chartreuse, or green; emerge in summer

KEY TO LARVAE OF TRICHOPTERA, caddis flies (*tricho*, hair; *ptera*, wing: referring to hairs that cover wings of adult)
KEY I, LARVA WITHOUT CASE
1a. Conspicuous, branched, filamentous gills on underside of abdomen (Fig. B-44), top of each thoracic segment covered with a single large, hard plate: family Hydropsychidae, net-spinning caddises; larvae build nets in fast water

Figure B-44. A Hydropsychidae caddis larva. *AL*=anal legs.

1b. Without gills on abdomen, top of middle and last thoracic segment without plates or each with several small plates . . . 2

    2a. Anal legs (*AL*) prominent, projecting well beyond last abdominal segment (see Fig. B-44), ninth abdominal segment with hard plate on upper surface, larvae are free-living and often bright green: family Rhyacophilidae, genus *Rhyacophila* (Green Rock Worm) (Fig. B-45); live in gravel bottoms of cold streams

Figure B-45. The larva of *Rhyacophila* spp. (Green Rock Worm).

2b. Anal legs prominent, but ninth abdominal segment lacking hard plate on upper surface: families Philoptoamidae, Psychomyiidae, and Polycentropodidae, all build long finger- or trumpet-shaped nets in the currents; the *Chimarra* caddises are found in the Philopotamidae; members of the Polycentrodidae are the most tolerant of any caddis to organic pollution such as sewage

KEY II, LARVA WITH CASE

1. Larva very small (average 3 mm), case variable (Fig. B-46) but larger than larva and often fastened to substrate, abdomen wider and/or deeper than thorax: family Hydroptilidae, microcaddises; lakes and streams

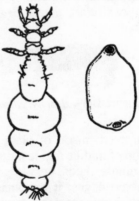

Figure B-46. A very common microcaddis larva *Leucotrichia pictipes)* and its tough, silken case. Case is actually much larger than larva and cemented to a stone in moving water.

2. Snail-shaped case of sand grains: family Helicopsychidae, genus *Helicopsyche;* gravel bottoms in fast water
3. Case of sand grains shaped like a turtle shell (Fig. B-47), ninth

segment of abdomen with hard plate on upper surface: family Glossostomatidae; gravel bottoms

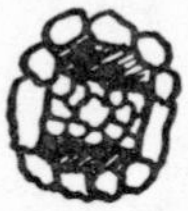

Figure B-47. Case of Glossostomatidae larva.

4. Case of sand grains with distinct flanges at sides and hooded in front (Fig. B-48), claws of hind legs small, those of other legs large: family Molannidae, genus *Molanna;* gravel bottoms

Figure B-48. Case of *Molanna* larva.

5. Case of plant fragments, square in cross section (occasionally round) and tapered like a chimney (Fig. B-49), larva often green: family Brachycentridae, genus *Brachycentrus*, American Grannom; gravel bottoms

Figure B-49. *Brachycentrus* larva in case.

6. Case long, tapered, made of plant fragments arranged in spiral (Fig. B-50), top of middle and last thoracic segments lacking plates or with only minute plates, very large larvae: family Phryganeidae, lakes and stream edges; if antennae are prominent and case as above, family Leptoceridae, genus *Triaenodes;* vegetation in moving water

Figure B-50. Spiral case of a Phryganeidae larva.

7. Case tapered, of sand grains, curved like a cornucopia, often with sticks along the side (Fig. B-51), top of middle thoracic segment with a pair of sickle-shaped plates, antennae are prominent: family Leptoceridae, includes White Miller and Black Dancer; gravel and vegetation in streams

Figure B-51. Case of Leptoceridae larva.

8. Case of sand with flanges of large pebbles attached at sides, top of middle thoracic segment with two distinct plates: family Goeridae and *Neophylax autumnus* of family Limnephilidae
9. Case of sand grains, slightly curved, uniform diameter throughout, outer forward edges of plate on top of first thoracic segment protracted into points (Fig. B-52), four plates on top of middle thoracic segment (2 small, 2 large), case easily crushed: family Sericostomatidae, genus *Agarodes;* sand and gravel bottoms

Figure B-52. Top of thorax of *Agarodes* larva, *P*=plate.

10. Same as 9 except: three plates on top of middle thoracic segment (Fig. B-53), case very hard; family Odontoceridae, genus *Psiloterta,* sand and gravel bottoms

Figure B-53. Top of thorax of *Psilotreta* larva.

11. Case log cabin type made of twigs or round one of pebbles, antennae very short and near eye, prominent spacing hump on top of

first abdominal segment (Fig. B-54): family Lepidostomatidae: clean streams

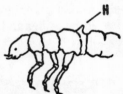

Figure B-54. Forepart of Lepidostomatidae larva showing spacing hump (*H*)

12. Case variable: log cabin type, of pebbles, or of plant fragments, antennae very short but located midway between eye and base of the mandible (Fig. B-55), no spacing hump on top of first abdominal segment: family Limnephilidae; lakes and pools, a few in swift water

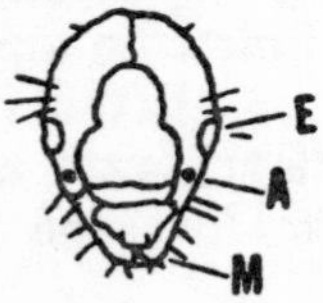

Figure B-55. Head of Limnephilidae larva: *E*=eye, *A*=antenna, (notice it is *very* short), *M*=mandible.

ANNOTATED BIBLIOGRAPHY

Atherton, John. (1951) 1971 edition. *The fly and the fish*. Freshet Press, Rockville Centre, NY. A classic in American fly fishing literature. This text established the modern concepts of impressionism in fly tying.

Bashline, James. 1973. *Night fishing for trout*. Freshet Press, Rockville Centre, NY. A most readable text on night fishing; filled with excellent information and delightful stories.

Bergman, Ray. (1938) 1976 edition. *Trout*. Alfred Knopf, New York. A masterpiece by a master angler. Contains a wealth of basic information on trout fishing.

Berners, Dame Juliana. C. 1496. "A treatyse of fysshynge wyth an angle." In *The Boke of St. Albans*, Westminster. The book that started it all. A text of considerable historical importance in fly fishing.

Brooks, Charles. 1970. *Larger trout for the western fly fisherman*. A. S. Barnes and Co., Cranbury, NJ. The first of Brooks's books. Filled with information on catching big trout on flies.

Brooks, Charles. 1974. *The trout and the stream*. Crown Publishers, New York. The best of Brooks's three books, this is a superb discussion of where trout are found and why.

Brooks, Charles. 1976. *Nymph fishing for larger trout*. Crown Publishers, New York. A fine book on nymphing in western waters. Best for its discussion of fishing large flies for big trout. Good information on aquatic organisms in western streams.

Brooks, Joe. 1968. *Complete book of fly fishing*. An Outdoor Life Book, A. S. Barnes and Co., New York. A basic primer for the fly fisher written by one of America's greatest anglers. Contains sound information on all phases of fly fishing.

Brooks, Joe. 1972. *Trout fishing*. Outdoor Life Books, Harper and Row, New York. Done as only Joe Brooks could do it, this text covers all the basics of fly fishing for trout: tackle, casting, playing the fish, stream tactics, and more. A classic.

Caucci, Al and Nastasi, Bob. 1975. *Hatches*. Comparahatch, New York. The single best book on mayflies that has been written for the angler. Excellent photographs.

Fox, Charles. 1967. *Rising trout*. The Telegraph Press, Harrisburg, PA. A collection of stories and tactics woven together in a delightful way. A book by a master trout fisherman.

Gordon, Sid. (1955). 1978 edition. *How to fish from top to bottom.* The Stackpole Company, Harrisburg, PA. A text that should be read by every serious fly fisher. This fine book will hone your ability to read the water and find trout.

Grant, George. 1971. *The art of weaving hair hackles for trout flies.* George Grant. Butte, MT. Good discussion of fly tying as done by one of the best.

Green, Jim. 1971. *Fly casting from the beginning.* Fenwick Corporation, Westminster, CA. An introductory text on fly casting and fly fishing equipment, this little paperback contains superb casting instructions by one of the best casters in the world.

Gregory, Myron. 1978. "Fly Lines." *Fly Fisherman Magazine,* vol. 9 (2): 52-58. A good article on fly lines with a bit of history by one of the men who made the history.

Grove, Alvin. (1951) 1971 edition. *The lure and lore of trout fishing.* Freshet Press, Rockville Centre, NY. This is an excellent text that must be studied again and again for it contains a real wealth of fly fishing information.

Hewitt, Edward R. (1948) 1972 edition. *A trout and salmon fisherman for 75 years.* Van Cortland Press, Croton-on-Hudson, NY. A good slice of early American trout fishing lore and history. Many of the lessons of this great father of nymph fishing in America are still pertinent.

Janes, Edward C. (ed.) 1970. *Fishing with Ray Bergman.* Alfred Knopf, New York. A collection of Bergman's angling columns. Positive advice from a great angler.

Koch, Ed. 1972. *Fishing the midge.* Freshet Press, Rockville Centre, NY. Devoted exclusively to fishing the tiny flies, this book is a must for the nymph fisher's library. Good discussions of tackle, techniques, and tying.

La Fontaine, Gary. 1976. *Challenges of the trout.* Mountain Press Publishing Company, Missoula, MT. Basic information on fly fishing for trout with some good biological insights into the behavior of trout and some of their food organisms.

Leisenring, James and Hidy, Vernon. 1971. *The art of tying the wet fly and fishing the flymph.* Crown Publishers, New York. A true classic by the father of wet fly fishing in America. A book that will never grow old.

McClane, A. J. (ed.) 1974. *McClane's new standard fishing encyclopedia and international angling guide.* Holt, Rinehart, and

Winston, New York. A massive, thorough volume that contains excellent information on all phases of fly fishing from how to do it to where to go. Good keys to mayflies and stoneflies.

Marinaro, Vincent. 1976. *In the ring of the rise.* Crown Publishers, New York. An exciting book with extraordinary photographs of feeding fish and marvelous insights into fly fishing.

Marsh, Ed. 1971. "A fly for all seasons." *Field and Stream*, vol. 75 (12): 38 ff. Describes the history and tying sequences for the South Platte Brassy.

Miller, Alfred (Sparse Gray Hackle). 1971. *Fishless days, angling nights.* Crown Publishers, New York. Dry wit is the order of the day (or is it the night?). A collection of delightfully humorous stories.

Nemes, Sylvester. 1975. *The soft hackled fly.* The Chatham Press, Old Greenwich, CT. A good discussion of this tying style and its place in the history and current practices of angling.

Quick, James. 1960. *Fishing the nymph.* Ronald Press Company, New York. The first book I ever owned on nymph fishing. This is a fine primer on this angling method. Contains good information on basic stream biology.

Ritz, Charles. (1959) 1972 edition. *A fly fisher's life.* Crown Publishers, New York. Ritz was one of the great fly fishers of modern times. This book is, quite simply, one of the best books on fly fishing, discussing tackle, casting, and techniques.

Rosborough, E. H. "Polly." (1965). 1978 edition. *Tying and fishing the fuzzy nymphs.* The Stackpole Company, Harrisburg, PA. A must for the nymph fisher. Read it over and over. This is a great book on fly tying.

Ross, H. H. (1944) 1972 edition. *The caddis flies or Trichoptera of Illinois.* Entomological Reprint Specialists, Los Angeles. A scientific treatise on caddis flies that contains much good biology that can be applied by the angler.

Sawyer, Frank. (1958) 1970 edition. *Nymphs and the trout.* Crown Publishers, New York. Sawyer is recognized as one of the pioneers of nymph fishing. This volume has a bit of history, a bit on tackle, and solid instruction on tying and fishing Sawyer's patterns.

Schwiebert, Ernest. 1961. "Early-season trout secrets." *Sports Afield*, vol. 145 (3): 43 ff. A fine article on early season fishing with nymphs and other flies.

Schwiebert, Ernest. 1973. *Nymphs*. Winchester Press, New York. *The book* on subaquatic forms found in trout streams of the United States. Also contains a treasure of nymphing information by one of the greatest anglers of our time.

Skues, G. E. M. 1949. *The way of a trout with a fly*. (4th ed.) A. and C. Black, London. A text that can never age because it contains so many basic insights into trout fishing. Skues is acknowledged as one of the great masters, and this book supports that opinion.

Skues, G. E. M. (1939) 1960 edition. *Nymph fishing for chalk stream trout*. A. and C. Black, London. Skues was the father of nymph fishing. All nymph fishers must read this classic book in which Skues describes his patterns and tactics.

Solomon, Larry and Leiser, Eric. 1977. *The caddis and the angler*. The Stackpole Company, Harrisburg, PA. An important book because it is the first angling text aimed exclusively at the caddis flies. Good discussions of life cycles, tackle, and tying techniques.

Swisher, Doug and Richards, Carl. 1971. *Selective trout*. Crown Publishers, New York. The book that established the no-hackle concept in modern fly tying. Also an authoritative study on mayfly hatches of the United States.

Swisher, Doug and Richards, Carl. 1975. *Fly fishing strategy*. Crown Publishers, New York. Discusses the concepts of stillborn flies and dry nymphs. Also a good primer on casting.

Walton, Izaak and Cotton, Charles. 1948 edition. *The compleat angler; or the contemplative man's recreation*. The Heritage Press, New York. For the fly fisher, Cotton's chapter is required reading.

Wendelburg, Tom. 1976. "How to read a trout stream." In *Trout Fisherman's Digest*, ed. by David Richey. DBI Books, Northfield, IL. A good discussion on reading the water.

ANNOTATED LIST OF REFERENCE TEXTS AND KEYS USED FOR IDENTIFICATION OF INVERTEBRATE FOOD ORGANISMS OF THE TROUT

Borror, D. J. and De Long, D. M. 1964. *An introduction to the study of insects.* Revised edition. Holt, Rinehart, and Winston, New York. Contains a good discussion of the biology of the various orders of insects, good keys, and fine drawings.

Burks, B. D. (1953) 1975 edition. *The mayflies or Ephemeroptera of Illinois.* Entomological Reprint Specialists, Los Angeles. A classic in entomological literature. Some scientific names are outdated, but the basic materials on structure and biology are sound.

Chu, H. F. 1949. *How to know the immature insects.* William C. Brown Company, Dubuque, IA. Strictly a key, but has good drawings.

Comstock, J. H. 1948. *An introduction to entomology.* (9th ed.) Comstock Publishing Company, Ithaca, NY. An in-depth introduction to insects.

Edmunds, G. F., Jr.; Jensen, S. L.; and Berner, L. 1976. *The mayflies of North and Central America.* University of Minnesota Press, Minneapolis. The latest and most complete work on American mayflies. Excellent drawings and keys to the genus level. Contains a great deal of biology that can be directly applied to angling.

Frison, T. H. 1942. "Studies of North American Plecoptera with special reference to the fauna of Illinois." *Bull. Ill. Nat. Hist. Survey,* vol. 22, article 2. A fine treatise on the stoneflies. Superb drawings and good biological data are very useful. Updates older classification schemes.

Hilsenhoff, W. L. 1975. *Aquatic insects of Wisconsin.* Technical Bulletin 89, Wisconsin Department of Natural Resources, Madison. Completely illustrated keys to genera of aquatic nymphs and larvae. Also contains some very good biological information. All scientific names are current.

Jacques, H. E. 1947. *How to know the insects.* William C. Brown Company, Dubuque, IA. A good key to major insect groups. Good drawings.

Jacques, H. E. 1951. *How to know the beetles.* William C. Brown Company, Dubuque, IA. Has good drawings of the various aquatic beetle larvae.

Leonard, Justin W. and Leonard, Fannie A. 1962. *Mayflies of Michigan trout streams.* Cranbrook Institute of Science, Bloomfield

Hills, MI. This classic work has served as a foundation for many anglers. Fine drawings and photographs complement the text. Some newer family names are not used in this text.

Merritt, R. W. and Cummins, K. W. (eds.) 1978. *An introduction to aquatic insects of North America.* Kendall/Hunt Publishing Company, Dubuque, IA. Very simply the best treatise available on structure of aquatic insects. Over 1,000 superb line drawings. Keys to families of adult and immature aquatic insects. A must.

Needham, J. G.; Traver, J. R.; and Hsu, Yin-Chi. (1935) 1972 edition. *The biology of mayflies.* E. W. Classey, Hampton, England. The authority on mayflies until the publication of the book by Edmunds *et al.*, this book contains a true wealth of information. Some scientific names are not current.

Pennak, R. W. 1953. *Fresh-water invertebrates of the United States.* Ronald Press, New York. The standard reference work in biology of freshwater invertebrates, this text contains good keys and excellent synopses of the biology of these organisms. Some scientific names have been changed since this book was published.

Ross, H. H. (1944) 1972 edition. *The caddis flies or Trichoptera of Illinois.* Entomological Reprint Specialists, Los Angeles. The most comprehensive treatise on the caddis flies. Includes keys and notes on the biology of caddises. Some scientific classification has changed since this text was published.

Swan, L. A. and Papp, C. S. 1972. *The common insects of North America.* Harper and Row, New York. Contains good accounts of the biology of the various orders of insects.

Usinger, R. L. (ed.) 1963. *Aquatic insects of California.* University of California Press, Berkeley, CA. Although aimed at California insects, the keys to genera are good for the entire United States. Excellent discussions of the biology of aquatic insects.

Wiggins, Glen B. 1977. *The larvae of the North American caddisfly genera (Trichoptera).* University of Toronto Press, Toronto, Canada. The most current work on the larvae of caddises. Keys are very good. There are no keys to adults. Illustrated with outstanding drawings.

INDEX

A Fly Fisher's Life. 33
A Trout and Salmon Fisherman for 75 Years. 80
Acroneuria stonefly. 145, 149
Adams Lake. 111–114
AFTMA. 20
Alderfly. 65, 131, 140
American Grannom. 101
Anatomy, of trout. 38–50
Annelida. 160
Annotated bibliography. 183–86
Annotated list of reference texts. 187–88
The Art of Tying the Wet Fly. 102
The Art of Tying the Wet Fly and Fishing the Flymph. 73
The Art of Weaving Hair Hackle for Trout Flies. 147
Atherton, John. 132, 140
Avon River. 107

Backing. 16–17, 34–35
Backswimmer. 144
Baetis mayfly. 155
Bashline, Jim. 95, 96
Beetle (aquatic). 65, 131, 140, 144
Belly boat. 85
Bend pool, fishing of. 59
Bergman, Ray. 80, 125
Berners, Dame Juliana. 107, 125
Big Hole River. 91
Big Spring Creek. 123
Biology of trout. 38–50
Black Dancer. 101
Blackfly. 68, 100
Blacknose Dace. 131
Black Willow Fly. 149
Bleaching fur. 142
Blending fur. 141
Blue Quill. 70
Blue Winged Olive. 73
Boaze, Ral. 149
Brachycentrus caddis. 101
Broadheads River. 102
Brooks, Charlie. 18, 133–35
Brooks, Joe. 93, 142
Brooks method. 133–35, 138, 139
Brown Drake. 144

Brule River. 73

The Caddis and the Angler. 99, 159
The Caddis Flies or Trichoptera of Illinois. 97
Caddisfly. 65, 67, 70, 90, 97–106, 110, 113, 145, 154
Caddis Midge. 157
Callibaetis mayfly. 113, 155
Casting. 26–37, 74–75
    accuracy. 37
    backhand. 34–35
    basic stroke. 26–27
    curve. 35
    double haul. 30–31
    of lead tip line. 138
    of long tippet. 122
    mending while. 31–33, 92–94
    overland roll. 28–29
    parachute. 33–34
    pickup and laydown. 29–30
    reach. 31
    roll. 27–28
    S-. 32
    shooting line. 30
    tension. 34, 138
Caucci, Al. 159
Challanges of the Trout. 100
Chironomidae midge. 110, 156
Coleoptera. 154, 162–63
The Compleat Angler. 117
Complex hatch. 70
Complex rise. 44
Compound rise. 43–44
Confluence line, fishing in. 60, 80
Cortland Line Company. 125
Cotton, Charles. 109, 117
Countdown method. 82
Cranefly. 65, 150
Crangonyx gracilis scud. 117
Cressbug. 120, 144, 145, 147
Crustacea. 116, 159
Currents
    eddying. 53–55, 57
    in lakes. 61
    in streams. 52–53, 57–58, 93

Dalnodar. Jim. 126
Dam. Royce. 152
Damselfly. 65, 87, 110, 113, 145
Diptera. 163–66
Dobsonfly. 65, 131, 140
Drag
    on line. 75–76
    on reel. 16
Dragonfly. 65, 87, 90, 110, 113
Drift. of aquatic organisms. 119
Dry nymph. 72
Dye formulas. 141

"Early-Season Trout Secrets." 78
Edges. as lies. 55–56
Emergers. 66, 72
Epeorus mayfly. 67, 140, 144
Ephemera mayfly. 144, 153
Ephemerella mayfly. 70, 73, 144, 154, 155
Ephemeroptera. 166–73
Epheron mayfly. 153
Equipment. 13–24

Falling Spring Creek. 73, 121
Fast rod. 84
Feeding lie. 55
Fenwick. 9, 26
Field and Stream magazine. 155
Fins. of trout. 49
Fisherman's Paradise. 84
Fishfly. 65, 131, 140
"Fishing and Flymph." 102
Fishing the Midge. 156
Fishing the Nymph. 118
Fishless Days, Angling Nights. 94
The Fly and the Fish. 140
Fly Casting from the Beginning. 26
Fly Fisher magazine. 9
Fly Fisherman magazine. 9, 20
Fly Fishing Strategy. 20, 21, 31, 65
Food web. in aquatic systems. 51
Fontaine. Ben. 20
Fox. Charles. 84, 90, 120

Gammarus limnaeus scud. 117
Garcia Corporation. 19
Gaumer. Dick. 9
Gee. Lacey. 151
Giant Black Stonefly. 149
Giant Michigan Mayfly. 144
Gimp. 151
Glare. on water. 41–42, 113
Gold Ribbed Hare's Ear. 144
Gordon. Sid. 105
Grant. George. 132, 147, 150
Gray Drake. 144
Gray Fox. 144
Green. Jim. 9, 26
Green Rock Worm. 99, 100, 149, 150
Gregory. Myron. 20
Griffith. George. 74
Griffith's Gnat. 74, 157–58
Grove. Alvin. 25–26

Hatches. 159
Hatching process. 65–70
Hair Leg Scud. 145–47
Hair Leg Wooly Worm. 133, 135, 144–45

Handling. of trout. 47–48
Hatching. of insects. 65–70
Harvey. George. 76, 84
Hearing. of trout. 45–46
Hemiptera. 173–74
Hendrickson. 70, 144
Henry's Fork. 73
Hewitt. Edward. 19, 80, 83, 118, 119, 125, 147
Hexigenia mayfly. 144, 153
Hidy. Vernon. 73, 102
Hoffnagle. Jerry. 9
Hooking. of fish. 76–77, 103, 134
Horse-Collar Midge. 84
How to Fish From Top to Bottom. 105
Hyallela azteca scud. 117
Hydraulic cushion. of stream. 53
Hydroptilidae caddis. 104
Hydropsychidae caddis. 98–100, 150

In the Ring of the Rise. 44
Insecta. 160–82
Impressionism. in artificials. 140–41
Isonychia mayfly. 65, 87, 144

Keeper of the Stream. 107
Keys to food organisms of trout. 159–82
    Annelida. 160
    Crustacea. 159
    Insecta. 160–82
        Coleoptera. 162–63
        Diptera. 163–66
        Ephemeroptera. 166–73
        Hemiptera. 173–74
        Lepidoptera. 174
        Megaloptera. 174–75
        Odonata. 175–76
        Plecoptera. 176–78
        Trichoptera. 178–82
    Mollusca. 160
Knots. 22–23, 136
Koch. Ed. 156, 157

LaFontaine. Gary. 100, 119
Lakes
    fishing in. 61–63, 82–83, 84, 111
    habitats of. 61–63
Large Mahogany Drake. 144
Larger Trout for the Western Fly Fisherman. 133
Latex caddis. 150
Laurel Run. 78
Leaders. 20–23, 75–76, 83–84, 109, 117–19, 128,
    135–37
Leisenring. Jim. 72–73, 102
Leisenring Lift. 74, 101–4, 133
Leiser. Eric. 99, 159
Lepidoptera. 131, 174
Letort Spring Creek. 123
Lies of the trout. 51–63
Life cycles. of insects. 97, 160
Line handling. 35–37
Lines. 17–20, 82–83, 137–38
Little Lehigh River. 102
Loop control. 30
Lunker Gazette magazine. 9
The Lure and Lore of Trout Fishing. 25, 26
Lynch. Gene. 155
Lyons. Nick. 9

Madison River. 91
Marinaro. Vince. 44
Marsh. Ed. 155

Masking hatch. 70
Mayfly. 65, 67, 87, 90, 110, 140, 144, 145, 154
McClane. A. J., 72, 159
*McClane's New Standard Fishing Encyclopedia and
  International Angling Guide*, 159
McCafferty. Bob. 90
Meanders in stream. 52
Mears. Sir Grimwood. 107
Megaloptera. 131–32, 174–75
Mending in the air. 31–32
Mending on the water. 32–33, 93, 94
Microcaddis. 104–5, 157
Microshot. 137
Midge. 65, 67, 69, 100, 113, 145, 154
Midge Nymph. 105, 156
Midge Pupa (fly). 113, 156–57
Miller. Alfred ("Sparce Gray Hackle"). 94–95
Moldable lead. 137
Mono Caddis Larva. 149–50
Mono Stonefly Nymph. 91, 135, 147–49
Monocular. 72
Moth (aquatic) 131, 140
Mountain midge. 68
Mueller. Ed. 84
Muscles. of trout. 49
Muskrat Nymph. 90, 113, 135, 151–52, 156
Mystacides sepulchralis caddis. 101

Nastasi. Bob. 159
Navajo Lake. 150
Nemes. Sylvester. 73, 93
Net Spinning Caddis. 150
Net-winged midge. 68
Night fishing. 94–96, 101
Night Fishing for Trout, 95
Nymph (defined). 11, 160–61
Nymph Fishing for Chalk Stream Trout, 64
Nymph Fishing for Larger Trout, 133
Nymphing tactics
    bottom bouncing. 118–22, 128, 136, 138
    Brooks method. 133–35, 138, 139
    during caddis hatch. 102–6
    down and across. 88–96
    fast rod. 84
    of the film. 64–77
    greased leader. 75
    greased line. 93–96, 104
    jumping nymph. 111–15, 122
    on lakes. 62–87, 111–15
    lead-tip line. 137–39
    Leisenring Lift. 101–4
    long tippet. 99, 116–22
    night fishing. 94–96, 101
    old standby. 88–96
    shotgunning. 127–30
    slow draw. 90
    on spring creeks. 90, 109–10, 120–26
    strike indicator. 119, 123–26, 128–30
    strip/tease. 78–87, 104, 153
    wingshooting (Sawyer's method). 107–15
Nymphs, 82, 149, 157, 159
Nymphs and the Trout. 107, 154

Odonata. 175–76
Overland roll cast. 28–29
O-ring/index finger pull. 35–36

Parachute cast. 33–34, 76
Paraleptophlebia mayfly. 70, 155
Pale Morning Dun. 154
Pelzl. Bob. 130

Perlidae stonefly. 149
Peshtigo River. 126
Pfiffer. Bill. 121
Pheasant Tail (Sawyer's). 113, 114, 154–55
Pils. Bob. 9, 131
Playing the fish. 16, 49–50
Plecoptera. 176–78
Plunge pool. fishing. 59–60, 80–81
Poly-Caddis. 90, 105
Pontoporeia affinis scud. 117
Pools. fishing. 56–59, 79–80, 84, 106, 120, 135
Potamanthus mayfly. 153
The Practical Fly Fisherman, 72
Presentation, of fly. 25
Prime lie. 55
Pteronarcys stonefly. 145, 149

Quick. Jim. 118
Quill Gordon. 67, 144

Rapids, fishing of. 55, 92–94, 138–39
Reach cast. 31, 76, 93, 94, 102, 138
Red Brown Nymph. 80, 113, 120, 124, 141–44
Reel. 16
Refraction. 39–43
Rhyacophila caddis. 99, 149
Richards. Carl. 20, 21, 31, 65, 66, 72, 142
Riffle hitch. 90, 96, 104
Riffles. fishing. 56, 80, 94, 127
Rise forms. 43–44
Rising Trout. 84
Ritz. Charles. 33
Rivers. large, fishing. 91
Rods
    action of. 14–15
    fixtures on. 15
    length of. 15–16, 85
    materials for. 13
    properties of. 13–14
Rosborough. Polly, 132, 141, 142, 149
Ross. Herbert. H., 97
Roundtable magazine. 9
Runs. fishing. 56

Salmo clarki trout. 88
San Juan River. 129
Sawyer. Frank, 107–8, 118, 122, 154
S-cast. 32
Scientific Anglers. 18, 19, 82
Schwiebert. Ernest. 78, 79, 82, 90, 149, 157, 158, 159
Scud. 89, 90, 113, 116–17, 120, 122, 144, 145–47, 150,
    156
Selectivity, of trout. 44
Selective Trout. 65, 142, 157
Senses, of trout. 38–50
Sheltering lie. 55
Shooting line (cast). 30
Shot (weight). 80, 128, 137
Silhouette of fly. 141
Silver Creek. 73, 122
Simple hatch. 70
Simple rise. 43
Siphlonurus mayfly. 65, 144
Skues. G. E. M., 64, 72, 74, 75, 102, 107, 108, 117,
    125
Slack. in line. 25–26, 76
Smell. trout's sense of. 46–47
Smith River. 119
Smutting rise. 70
The Soft Hackled Fly. 73
Solomon. Larry. 99, 159

South Platte Brassy. 110. 113. 155–56
South Platte River. 155
Sports Afield magazine. 78
Spring creek tactics. 90. 109–10. 120–26
Standing wave. in stream. 54–55
Stenonema mayfly. 144
Stewart. W. C.. 102
Stillborns. 66. 72
Stomach pump. 23
Stonefly. 65. 144
Stream log. importance of. 24
Stream. configuration of. 52–55
Strike indicator. 75. 119. 123–30
Strip Nymph. 152–53
Sun glasses. 23
Surface screen. sampling with. 24. 71. 105
Swisher. Doug. 20. 21. 31. 65. 66. 72. 142

Tailing trout. 108
Taste. trout's sense of. 46–47
Touch. trout's sense of. 47–48
Trichoptera. 178–82
Tricorythodes mayfly. 121
The Trout and the Stream. 18. 133
Trout Fishing. 142
Trout Unlimited. 74
Trueblood. Ted. 11
Turbulent flow (eddying). 53
Tying and Fishing the Fuzzy Nymphs. 141

Undercut banks. 59

Vegetation (aquatic). fishing near. 60–61. 86. 114
Vermejo Park Ranch. 111
Vision. of trout. 38–45

Walton. Izaac. 117. 125
Water. properties of. 38–39. 41–42. 51
Waterboatman. 85. 110. 113. 144
Waterfalls. fishing near. 59–60. 80
Watershed. 51
Web of life. 61
Wendelburg. Tom. 54
West. Howard. 9
Wet/Dry Fly. 72–74. 90. 153–54
White River. 80. 117
White Winged Black. 121
Whitlock. Dave. 9. 118. 125. 142
Window. of trout (vision). 40–43
Wingshooting tactic. 107–15
Wink underwater. 75. 108
Wiskowski. Russell. 95. 131
Woods. Arthur. 92
Wooly Worm. 90. 113. 131–39. 144–45
Wulff. Lee. 19

Yellow Breeches Creek. 123
Young. Paul. 147
Yellowstone River. 73. 88. 89. 91